U.S. Korea Talks & Me Too

U.S. Korea Talks & Me Too

by
Oscar Valdes

Copyright © 2018 by Oscar Valdes

All rights reserved. No part of this publication may be reproduced, distributed or transmitted in any form or by any means, including photocopying, recording, digital scanning or other electronic or mechanical methods, without the prior written permission of the publisher, except in the case of brief quotations embodied in critical reviews and certain other noncommercial uses permitted by copyright law.

This book is a production of Editorial Madruga,
P.O. Box 78, Pasadena, CA 91102

You may visit the author online at oscarvaldes.net.

Library of Congress Control Number: 2018940827

Published 2018
Printed in the United States of America
Print ISBN: 978-0-9793558-7-5
E ISBN: 978-0-9793558-8-2

Cover and interior design by Ann Valdés

For my daughter
&
for Masashi, Eneida, Craig and Priscilla, Jose M., JRL and Larry.

Thanks for the good times.

Dear Mr Trump,

Your much anticipated meeting with the leader of North Korea is fast approaching. Thinking of the possibilities, I have written these pages in an attempt to better understand the complexities involved.

You will be surrounded, of course, by advisers with great knowledge. Please take in their counsel and let it permeate your judgment.

Whatever decisions you may consider, let them be suffused with humanity, for many people's lives are at stake – both on our side and theirs.

As in all matters of great weight, do not forget that reflection is your best friend, rashness your worst enemy.

Good luck.

Oscar Valdes
Concerned Citizen

1

1/1/2018

Kim Jong-un states on North Korean Television, that "the entire US is within range of our nuclear weapons and a nuclear button is always on my desk. This is reality, not a threat. The weapons will be used only if our security is threatened." He added that it was imperative to lower military tensions on the Korean peninsula and improve ties with the South. He would consider sending a delegation to the Winter Olympics in Pyeongchang in February.

"North Korea's participation in the Games will be a good opportunity to show unity of the people and we wish the Games will be a success. Officials for the two Koreas may urgently meet to discuss the possibility."

South Korea's president, Moon Rae-in, welcomed the offer.

1/2/18

President Trump answers Kim Jong-un. He tweets, "will someone from his depleted and food starved regime please inform him that I, too, have a nuclear button, but it is a much bigger and more powerful one than his."

(There is no nuclear button, but a briefcase instead, called the nuclear football, carried by military personnel, and that follows the president wherever he goes. Should it be necessary, the president provides a code, "the biscuit", and weapons are fired from America's vast arsenal of nuclear weapons.)

Washington DC

The White House. Evening. Donald and Melania in their suite. They're both seated at a table.

Melania (irritated) - I don't get why you replied as you did.
Donald - Had to put him in his place.
Melania - He was stating the facts, wasn't he? 'We have the weapons. Leave us alone'.
Donald - He's grandstanding.
Melania - Their long-range missiles may or may not carry a nuclear warhead that can hit us, but there's no doubt they can now hit South Korea and Japan. So they are already a nuclear power.
Doanld - I will not allow it.
Melania - But it's beyond you.
Donald - We'll see.
Melania (calmly) - Dee… Kim stated a fact.
Donald - They are a depleted and food starved regime…
Melania - With nuclear weapons! And he is saying that he wants to be left alone, so they can get on with their economic development.

She gets up and crosses to the window. She turns around to face him.

Melania - What is wrong with what he's asking?
Donald - He does not have our consent.
Melania - What? Did China have our consent? Did Russia or Pakistan get it?
Donald - No.

Melania - So why does North Korea need it?
Donald - They're a ruthless and unpredictable regime.
Melania - Ruthless you say… do we have any control over how ruthless China or Russia are being with their people, as we speak?
Donald - Excuse me, but did you know that in 1987, the year before Seoul staged the Summer Olympics, North Korean agents blew up a Korean Air passenger plane, killing all 115 passengers aboard?
Melania - Dee, I'm not saying they're not ruthless… or not unpredictable… but isn't that why the "nuclear football" follows you everywhere you go? Any nation can be unpredictable… and we have to live with that.
Donald - So you want us to put up with a little ill-tempered bully right next to South Korea and Japan?
Melania - Why not? He has to live with you, you and your temper tantrums.
Donald - My temper tantrums?
Melania - Yes.

She turns back to look out the window.

Melania - The things you say, Dee… so impulsive… not what a statesman would say.
Donald - I have my own style.
Melania - Not that you couldn't become a statesman… but it seems there's a part of you that refuses to grow up and become one.

Donald gets up and walks to join her by the window. They look out into the DC evening.

Melania - From what I've read, experts are skeptical that

nuclear proliferation can ever be stopped. Someone said that critical information and designs can be loaded into a thumb drive. How're you going to stop that?
Meanwhile, India is collaborating with Russia to develop cruise missiles. India and North Korea are working on submarine launched missiles. Iran has been working on the weapons and they will have them eventually… sanctions or no sanctions… because people with the know-how and expertise will be willing to sell it… and smuggle it in, in a thumb drive.
Donald - Not on my watch. We're able inspect their sites. At least that was accomplished. But I may want to scrap the deal anyway.
Melania - Any country smart enough and determined enough will get nuclear weapons, if they want to.
And we have to live with it.
(looking him in the eye)
Dee… what happened to diplomacy?

He looks off.

Melania - The lives that would be lost if war were to break out… the pain… the suffering…
Donald (skeptically) - Look at all the diplomacy we did with North Korea over the years. They sat at the negotiating table all right, but they just kept lying. Signing agreements, like the one that Jimmy Carter negotiated for Bill Clinton in '94…
Melania - With Kim's father… Kim Jong-il.
Donald - … nodding and smiling… while continuing to build their weapons. Didn't miss a beat.
Melania - But they didn't harm us, did they?
Donald - We imposed sanctions but China and Russia traded with them, anyway.
Melania - They have a history, those three… and their regimes

are not that different… so they feel closer to each other than to us.

Donald looks down at the ground and clasps his hands.

Melania - I'm sure Kim looks at South Korea and wonders if North Korea can ever develop as much.
Donald - North Koreans keep defecting to the South.
Melania - Something's wrong with their system and they know it. They know they have to work on the economy.

Melania draws closer to Donald and circles his waist, resting her head on his chest.

Melania - There's the risk of overreacting…
Donald - That, there is.
Melania - … And if we're not measured it can be very bad.

Donald wraps his arms around her. They remain there for a moment, rocking lightly from side to side.

Donald - Tell you what… I'm going to think about diplomacy… Jim in Defense favors it… and see what I can come up with.

2

1/10/18

Trump tweets - The single greatest Witch Hunt in American history continues. There was no collusion, everybody including the Dems knows there was no collusion, & yet on and on it goes. Russia and the world is laughing at the stupidity they are witnessing. Republicans should finally take control!

Trump tweets - Cutting taxes and simplifying regulations makes America the place to invest! Great news as Toyota and Mazda announce they are bringing 4,000 JOBS and investing $1.6 BILLION in Alabama, helping to further grow our economy.

Washington DC

The Oval Office. Evening. Donald is at his desk. The phone rings.

Secretary - Mr President?
Donald - Yes?
Secretary - South Korea's President wishes to speak with you.
Donald - Put him through.
Moon - Good evening Mr Trump…
Donald - Oh, please, call me Donald, I insist. And good morning to you.
Moon - Thank you.
Donald - You always do that, you know, start with calling me Mr Trump… forgetting what I've told you before… we have to put

an end to it.
Moon (laughs) - Very well. This will be the last time.
Donald - Good.
Moon - About postponing the military exercises we had scheduled...
Donald - I'm fine with that.
Moon - Great. That is very good news. North Korea has agreed to have their players join ours in the Olympic hockey team, so it will be one team.
Donald - You invited them?
Moon - Yes. We are to march under one flag, the blue flag representing our country united.
Donald - I'm sure there's going to be players that resent being bumped for political reasons.
Moon - Bumped?
Donald - Yeah, players that had been preparing for a long time and now will be sitting on the bench, watching instead.
Moon- I see. We'll try to get everyone to play a little. Good point.
Donald - You think the marching together will help ticket sales?
Moon (laughs) - I think it may.
Donald - If it does, then we're good. Got to keep looking at the bottom line.
Moon - Yes, of course.
Donald - Moon, what about reunification... let's be honest... isn't that just a pipe dream?
Moon - No, I don't think so.
Donald - But how is that going to work out, South Korea a democracy and the North a dictatorship? I'm sure Kim won't want to let go of his position.
Moon - I don't know either... but we are one people, Donald... one people... and we have to keep working at it. As for South Korea, we'll never give up our democracy.

Donald - And he won't give up his communism.
Moon - But my hope is that… like in China… Kim will open the markets and they will see the benefits of trading.
Donald - Follow the Chinese model?
Moon - Yes… the Chinese model as a stage… not as an end in itself. I'm not in favor of their police state. But with prosperity… maybe the border that divides us will be opened one day.
Donald - Like in Germany.
Moon - Yes.
Donald - We'll have to see… but frankly, I'm pessimistic… I don't think it will ever happen.
Moon - We must have patience, Donald… lots of patience… and show them our ways are better than theirs. It will take years… but my dream is that one day it will happen.

3

The next day. The White House. The Oval office. Donald is seated by the fireplace, along with generals John Kelly and Jim Mattis.

Donald - Will Kim accept dismantling his nuclear weapons program, in exchange for the removal of sanctions?
Mattis - I don't think so.
Kelly - I agree.
Mattis - They've worked very hard at it… and now… like it or not, they're a nuclear power.
Donald - We managed to put a halt to Iran's program…
Kelly - But Iran wasn't as far along as North Korea, plus they weren't next to Russia and China… and they had Israel on them, watching all the time, with the very clear objective of not letting them make the bombs. Israel's survival was at stake.
Mattis - Maybe we weren't as committed to denuclearization in North Korea, for whatever reason, and they overcame the obstacles.
Kelly - Why are we now so invested that North Korea denuclearize? Is Kim more of a threat than Xi or Putin?
Mattis - Are we tangled up in the notion that, having cheated us all along, they must now, finally, surrender? Is it a matter of pride? Look how confident Kim is. It comes from the sense that he's become a nuclear power and his belief that it makes him a world leader, who now has the means to allay fears, real or imagined, that we will want to depose him.
Kelly - On the tip of his missiles, he's probably had his name printed.
Donald - He's not a world leader.

Kelly - But having the weapons he can demand the world's attention.
Donald - Why do you think he's now wanting to talk?

Kelly and Mattis look at each other.

Mattis - I think the sanctions are biting… but he's also seized on the fact that there's chaos in the White House.

Donald nods pensively.

Kelly - Whatever the flaws of the Iran nuclear deal, we would not have been able to pull it off if the White House had not been stable.
Donald - John, please don't compare me to Obama.
Mattis - But he's right… and unpleasant as it may be, you have to face it.
Donald - Believe me, I would've got a better deal for us.

Donald gets up, crosses to the window and stands there as he looks out.

Donald - This Russia thing has gone on too long… it has been a huge distraction.
Mattis - It's contributed to your making poor choices. Owning up to them is the first step to correcting them.
Donald - Jim, give me one poor choice…
Mattis - Okay, take Kushner for instance… what experience does this guy have, for you to give him such say in Middle East matters? Just because you feel comfortable with him does not justify the assignment.
Kelly - Kim is wily, if nothing else, and he sees the disarray and wants to exploit it.

Mattis - Add to it, Mr President, that you're an open book. Our system being what it is, open and uncensored, every flaw of yours gets full exposure… the opposition makes sure of that. Kim, on the other hand, is ultra secretive. He knows all about you but you know nothing about him. So, on the world stage, he comes across as composed and focused, while you present yourself as disorganized and impulsive.

Donald returns to his seat, alongside the generals.

Mattis (to Trump) - Say, for example, that Kim announced that he wanted to talk directly to you… which you had mentioned as a possibility at some point during the campaign. Should you agree, it would be a win for him… just drawing you to the table.
Kelly - If you were to ask him that he dismantle his weapons, he'd want those sanctions pulled back.
Donald - Wouldn't trust him.
Mattis - Nothing short of a Marshall plan for North Korea would do, but he keeps his repressive apparatus in place.
Donald - Nope, no Marshall plan with him in power, I can assure you that. I just don't think he'll ever dismantle… it's all posturing.
Kelly - For the sake of the discussion… if he were to offer dismantling of his nuclear program… he would want to tell us where and when the nuclear inspectors would go to verify the process… and he'll laugh at us, right in front of everybody.
Mattis - Let alone that there's no certain way of verifying where the warheads are.

Donald sits back and folds his arms.

Donald - The fact that he has nuclear weapons doesn't make

him a world power.
Kelly - Of course not.
Mattis - There's the added problem that any perception of weakness on your part, will embolden Iran further.
Kelly - Mr President, no matter how confident you may be in your negotiating skills… this stands to be a tough fight.

Donald leans forward, arms on his knees, hands joined together.

Mattis - Mr President, I think you're feeling an enormous pressure to perform… and performing is integral to your showman personality… but performing for performing's sake doesn't cut it at this level.
Kelly - The chaos here in the White House goes on.
Donald - John, didn't I bring you in to handle that?
Kelly - I've got my hands full, sir.

Donald looks at both his generals in the eye.

Donald - I appreciate your honesty… both of you… and I would be burying my head in the sand if I said I was not the chief maker of the chaos… and truth be told I enjoy it… keeps me at center stage… but I agree that it's not what's best for the office… or for the country.

Kelly and Mattis nod.

Donald - Of all the challenges I've faced… and I've faced many… this is the greatest one… the presidency… because it forces me to square with myself and my flaws. I could not do the job without all the help I'm getting… that's all too clear… which has got me to wondering if I shouldn't ask for another kind of help… personal help.

Kelly and Mattis glance at each other.

Donald - I've given some thought to this idea but wanted to run it by you… in the strictest of confidence, of course. So, gentlemen… given that I want to become a better president… and that I'm in it for the long run… do you think I should see a psychiatrist?

Taken by surprise, Kelly and Mattis stare back at Donald.

Kelly - Mr President… with all due respect… I think it will help.
Mattis - It would not take anything away from your multiple talents and may help your decision making.
Kelly - We all have private demons that get in the way. For sure, Kim, Xi and Putin, all could use a psychiatrist, and a lot more than you do.
Mattis - They're repressing millions of people to satisfy their ambitions.
Kelly - Exactly.

Donald smiles to himself as he nods pensively.

Donald - Back to the North Korean problem… unrealistic expectations have been raised…

Kelly and Mattis both look down at the ground.

Donald - What if… we let North Korea keep their nuclear weapons?

Kelly and Mattis look intrigued by the idea.

Donald - Will the world see it as a great defeat for America?

Mattis - Some people will… but I don't think so.
Donald - John?
Kelly - I agree.
Donald - Why?
Kelly - It's accepting reality. Realpolitik.
Mattis - Stated or not, North Korea has been China's and Russia's proxy in their antagonism with the West.
Kelly - And so they have helped Kim circumvent the sanctions.
Mattis - North Korea lies within their camp… their nuclear weapons all pointed at us.

Donald stands and begins to pace.

Donald - And so… as an idea… what if we put it on them… on China and Russia?
Mattis - What do you mean?
Donald - I say to China and Russia, you denuclearize North Korea… and until you do, we'll put nuclear weapons in South Korea. When America is assured that there are no more weapons in North Korea, we'll remove them from the South.

Kelly and Mattis look at each other.

Mattis - Interesting.
Kelly - It's an option.
Mattis (to Kelly) - You think South Korea will object to it?
Kelly - I don't think so, but for sure China and Russia will.
Donald - And that's just too bad.

Donald sits back down.

Donald - Up the ante. This is the time to do it, gentlemen. Share the pain. MAD. Mutual Assured Destruction.

Mattis - China and Russia will say they have no control over North Korea.
Donald - They helped create a bellicose North Korea, didn't they? Time to pay the piper.

Mattis rises and walks to the window, stands there for a moment, then turns around to face Donald and Kelly.

Mattis - It's a valid option.
Donald - And in the meantime… we keep the sanctions. North Korea can keep making weapons if they want to, and we blockade them, make sure they don't get out, see who wins the game. They're the ones who are starving, not us. Ours is the economy that produces, not theirs. That's how we won the Cold War.

Donald stands and walks over to join Mattis by the window. Kelly gets up and follows, so it's the three men huddled together.

Donald - Having said that… I'll be more than glad to call up Kim… and ask that we meet in secret. Just so I can get a feel for the man.
Mattis - I like it.

Kelly nods in agreement.

Donald put his hands on the two generals' shoulders.

Donald - Back to the psychiatrist issue, should I move forward with the idea… do I keep it a secret or not?
Mattis (smiling) - I would make it public from the get go. Better than the press finds out.
Kelly - You would get plenty of flak… that's for sure… but it

would be a heck of a stunt.

Donald - Will it help my ratings?

Mattis - I wouldn't know… but you can handle controversy.

Donald looks out the window, the mood thoughtful.

Donald - On the other hand… I could just buy a book on what it is that psychiatrists actually do… and take it from there.

Kelly and Mattis look puzzled.

Donald - Maybe I'll do that first. Gentlemen, I appreciate your help. Thank you.

The men shake hands and the generals exit. Donald remains by the window, looking out into the DC afternoon.

4

Sometime thereafter, as the tensions between the US and North Korea deepened, Donald Trump proposed to meet secretly with Kim Jong-un. The North Korean leader accepted. Days later, Trump flew to an undisclosed location in North Korea.
In the center of a large room, the two men sit near each other, at an angle, two small coffee tables in front of them, a bottle of water and a glass each.
A distance behind, two American generals stand near Trump, and two North Korean generals stand near Kim.

Donald - Well, here we are.
Kim - Yes. You read about me?
Donald - There's not much written about you.
Kim - You're opposite. Too much written about you. Don't know where to begin.
Donald - It's the free press… so called free press, I should say… they're really a bunch of troublemakers, but they're protected by the first amendment.
Kim - Right to express yourself…
(he shakes his head)
Not good. In my country, I express for everybody. Like Xi in China… and Putin in Russia. It's simpler that way.
Donald - I like simpler… no fake news.
Kim (laughs) - No fake news. You make that up, don't you?
Donald - That's right. I made it popular.
Kim - A lot of people don't love you in your country.
Donald - People that matter love me… people who go out and vote.
Kim (shaking his head) - No elections in North Korea. My

family knows best. My father was leader, his father was leader.
Donald - I want Ivanka to be the next president.
Kim - Oh, yes, very pretty. She get elected. Everybody vote for her.
Donald - Thank you.
Kim - What about sons?
Donald - They run hotel business.
Kim - Very good. Keep it in family.
Donald - That's right.
Kim - Good hotel?
Donald - Excellent. The best.
Kim - Why you not build hotel in North Korea?
Donald - Well, you don't have a lot of visitors.
Kim - You build, people come. I tell people, 'go to hotel. Hotel is good', people go.
Donald - Thank you.
Kim - I come, too.
Donald - Thank you.
Kim - I read New York Times, in Chinese. Very interesting how people talk about you. Here in North Korea, that is sign of disrespect.
Donald - I agree.
Kim - First amendment?
Donald - That's it.

One of the American generals approaches Trump, leans in.

General (sotto voce) - Mr President, remember we're here to discuss nuclear weapons.
Donald - I got it.

The General returns to his position.

Donald - So, Kim… can I call you Kim?
Kim - Sure. I call you Donald.
Donald - Good. Excellent start. Why are you building so many nuclear weapons?
Kim - You make threat.
Donald - That's because you're firing the missiles.
Kim - You try to kill us.
Donald - Why would I want to do that?
Kim - To show everybody you number one in world.
Donald - But we are number one, Kim, that's a fact.
Kim - For now. But you start fading. You say, 'America First', so you pull back from the world. China laugh and say, better for us, we fill the space. Chinese export more than you, manufacture more than you… in few years, more technology than you. Smart people go to China instead.
Donald - Not going to happen.
Kim - You wait.
Donald - Kim, let's look at the present… we have the most weapons right now.
Kim - Yes… but I can put missile in California.
Donald - Yes… (to himself) a blue state too…
Kim - Blue?
Donald - Never mind. Kim… you know I can destroy you.
Kim - You can, but your people not forgive you… you don't get elected again.
Donald - Actually, it would be easier, one blue state less.
Kim - What?
Donald - Democrats… they're blue, republicans are red.
Kim - Oh, yes. Red like worker's party
Donald - Well, yes… come to think about it… but it's just a color.
Kim - Color important. Red is color of passion, energy, drive, strength, power.

Donald - That's right. We Republicans have all that. Which is why we won the election.
Kim - Why you threaten North Korea?
Donald - Because you threaten us.
Kim - No. You threaten me first.
Donald - Kim, no… look… it's very dangerous to be using threats… I mean… I recognize that I've done that but… it could get us into trouble.

Kim nods.

Donald - See, if there is so much distrust… a mistake could be made… and you would think you were being attacked and fire your missiles… but then we'd have all kinds of missiles coming to you… and there would be no place where you could hide. Do you understand that?
Kim - I have special bunker, for me and my family… have plenty of food. Everything. And I would be immortal… because my missiles hit San Francisco… and Google, Apple, Facebook… all down… and if I die, not matter, because the world recognizes me. I immortal.
Donald - Kim… brother…
Kim - Brother…?
Donald - It's an expression… way of being friendly…
Kim - Brothers sometimes kill each other.
Donald - True. But see… eventually, we would track you down and it wouldn't be pretty… do you understand?
Kim - Not pretty?
Donald - Another expression. When we find you, it would not be good.
Kim - I not wait for you to kill me. I do like Hitler, use poison pill. I die listening to great music… Tchaikovsky…. Rachmaninov… knowing San Francisco burning… like Rome…

out of picture.
Donald - Dude…
Kim - Dude?
Donald - Just an expression… friendly… very friendly.
Kim - Good.
Donald - Kim… I've come all the way here because Melania suggested it.
Kim - Your wife?
Donald - Yes.
Kim - Very pretty. Classy.
Donald - Thank you. She's rubbing off on me…
Kim - Rub off?
Donald - Influencing me…
Kim - You let wife influence you?
Donald - I mean, we live together, we talk… sometimes… and she's strong willed…
Kim (laughs) - I just kidding… my wife influence me, too.
Donald - Great. Good to know that. Kim… brother… as I was saying… I've come all the way here… because I wanted you to see, for yourself, that I'm not crazy.

Kim stares at him.

Donald - That's right, Kim. I am not crazy. I have never been crazy. I want you to understand that.
Kim - You, not crazy?
Donald - Not at all.

Kim is skeptical.

Donald - I act crazy.
Kim - I saw your TV program.
Donald (pleasantly surprised) - You did?

Kim - You crazy.
Donald - No, no, Kim. Just an act... so people tune in...
Kim -Tune in?
Donald - Yes... so they watch... and I make money.
Kim - I see you and I want to have TV program, too.
Donald (with relief) - Oh, man... just say the word... I can set you up any day... I've got the producers... everything... I mean, just tell me when you're ready... we could go global.
Kim (smiling broadly) - I let you know.
Donald - Please do. Kim... a crazy man would not have been able to build all the hotels I've built. It takes some brains... not the greatest but some brains... to put it all together, you understand what I'm saying? You follow me?
Kim - No, I don't follow you. I stay right here, do my thing.
Donald - Kim, I'm sorry, that was just another expression.

Kim laughs.

Kim - Send me teacher so I learn all expressions.
Donald - I will do that... I will send you not just one but two teachers. Three teachers.
Kim - Thank you.
Donald - You're welcome. So, like I was saying, I am not crazy... it's an act that I put on.
Kim - Act?
Donald - Yes. I pretend... like in the TV show... so I keep people guessing... and my base...
Kim - Base?
Donald - People who voted for me... they love it. They were so fed up with everything... globalization, world moving too fast, immigrants coming into our country... that they were getting dizzy and they wanted someone crazy enough to say, stop everything! Protect us from the world! Put in tariffs! Climate

change? It's a trick. Bring back coal. 'America First!'

Kim frowns at Donald.

Donald - That's how I became president. By acting crazy... but I'm not crazy. (to himself) And I brought show business right into the presidency, didn't I?
Kim (looks off, the mood pensive) - You think I crazy?
Donald - No.
Kim - What you think of me?
Donald - I think you're acting crazy, like me, to please your base.
Kim (nods) - We both acting crazy?
Donald - Yes.
Kim (folding his arms, the expression glum) - Sometimes... I have to be crazy.
Donald - I know what you mean.
Kim (smiles now) - Everyone think you going to lose control, everyone fear you.
Donald - That's the best, when people fear you.
Kim - Better than people love you... but that good too.
Donald - Kim... I firmly believe... that if you and I get to know each other... that we will avoid a nuclear catastrophe. I mean, you and me talking... sharing personal things... if we do that, then we will see that we are not very different... that we are really just people...
Kim (doubtfully) - Just people?
Donald - I mean, very special people...

Kim nods approvingly.

Donald - ... who want to rule our nations until we die... and then let our heirs take over and so on.
Kim -Yes.

Donald - Do you want to rule until you die?
Kim - Yes. You?
Donald - Me too.
Kim - Me too? That women movement… very angry.
Donald - It will pass.
Kim - Why you think?
Donald - They'll get tired.
Kim (shaking head, doubtfully) - I think women come after you, form political party, send you back to New York.
Donald - Kim, believe me, I've got it under control.
Kim - Your wife under control?
Donald - Well, not exactly.
Kim - You can't control your wife, then Me Too movement grow and kick you out. I don't have that problem here. That's why I say you weak.
Donald - What?
Kim - Woman live with you but you can't control, that weak.
Donald - Kim, I am not weak. I am strong. Look, Hillary Clinton had all that experience, plus the advice of her husband, the support of Obama, a lot more money than me, and I beat her.
Kim - How you do that?
Donald (grins) - Acting crazy.

Kim laughs.

Donald - People loved it. They said, 'that crazy man is strong'.
Kim - They say same thing here, Kim crazy to challenge America, but Kim strong.
Donald - People don't like to think… they prefer emotion… so I give it to them.
Kim - Very true. I do same.
Donald - But now Americans are getting scared… with the

missiles you're firing…
and I have to do something.
Kim - My people scared, too… you talk crazy… you hold military exercise right off my coast… so I challenge you.
Donald - Kim… I'm bigger than you…
Kim (stiffening) - You not bigger.
Donald - Yes, I am.
Kim - No, you not!

The 4 generals in back of the room take a step front.

Donald pulls back in his seat for a moment.

Donald - Look, man… you can challenge me all you want, but that's all you can do, because if you keep firing the missiles, I will wipe you out. And then South Korea will take over.
Kim - I wipe out South Korea and San Francisco.

The two men look front. Communication has been broken.
One American general in the background approaches and leans in to speak to Donald.

General - Sir, please try another tack.
Donald - I got it.

The general returns to his position.

Kim - You say you not feminist?
Donald - I did say that.
Kim - Not smart for you to say that. Me Too movement will use against you.
Donald - Okay, how would you have handled it?
Kim - Say you sorry.

Donald laughs.

Kim - You never say you sorry for what you say or do. That not good. You never say I sorry for what pain you cause people.
Donald - Wait a minute. You're a dictator. When someone says or does something that bothers you, you take them out.
Kim - Take them out?

Donald runs his finger slowly across his throat.

Kim (smiles) - North Korea different than America. People know what to expect. But sometimes I say I'm sorry. To my friends, to my wife.
Donald (surprised) - You have friends?
Kim - I do. No man is island. Xi has friends. Putin has friends. You have friends?
Donald - I do.
Kim - You say sorry sometimes?

Donald looks off, wondering when was the last time he said he was sorry to someone other than Melania, and that, under duress.

Kim - You never say sorry that you call me Little Rocket Man.

Donald appears contrite. He was not expecting this from Kim.

Donald (trying to find the words) - I said that in a moment of anger… that's all… I was angry.

Kim keeps looking at him.

Donald - I forget what it was you had said… and I was really angry. That's all it was.

Kim stays looking at Donald.

Donald - But you can just dismiss it.

Kim doesn't take his eyes off Donald.

Donald (in frustration) - Okay, Okay! I'm sorry I called you Little Rocket Man! I'm sorry.

Kim smiles a big smile.

Donald - But you called me "a mentally deranged US dotard."
Kim - I did.
Donald - Are you sorry?
Kim - I'm sorry.

Donald smiles. Kim does too.

Kim - You feel better?
Donald - I do. Kim… except for me… why haven't you met with any foreign leader? Not even with Xi?
Kim - Complicated question.
Donald - You scared?
Kim - Kim not scared of anybody.
Donald - You know, it's okay to feel scared sometimes…
Kim - You scared sometimes?
Donald - Oh yeah.
Kim - When?
Donald - During the campaign… the debates…
Kim - I watch debates.
Donald - You did?

Kim - You crazy.
Donald - But it was an act… and they went for it. Before every debate I was scared, but I went in any way, and made fun of everybody. Made it up as I went along, like on my TV show. But look, if you get out a bit… it would be good for you.
Kim - I afraid I get kidnapped.
Donald - Hmm… that is a possibility. But you could go to China…
Kim - Not trust.
Donald - Okay… well… you can invite people to come see you.
Kim - I think about it.
Donald - You okay with me visiting, right?
Kim - Yes.
Donald - It wasn't easy. When I talked to my generals about it, they all said no.
Kim - They afraid I kidnap you?
Donald - No, of course not. So I insisted. And they finally agreed. (to himself) Maybe they saw a chance of getting rid of me?
Kim - What?
Donald - Never mind, just a thought. You know how all this started?
Kim - Harvey Weinstein.
Donald - What? No. That has nothing to do with it. Or… maybe. But no. It started when I made a promise to Melania.
Kim - Your wife?
Donald - That's right. She says the presidency has brought out the worst in me, so she wants me to do only one term and then go back to New York. Of course, I disagree, I'm just growing into the job. So I said, 'honey, what could I do to convince you that I have what it takes to be a statesman'?
Kim - Statesman?
Donald - A leader the world recognizes as visionary.

Kim nods wistfully.

Donald - And she said, 'take the initiative and go visit Kim. Surprise us with something that makes sense and shows you as a thinker.' She believes tweeting is not good for deep thinking.
Kim - Your wife smart.
Donald - Thank you. Oh, and she sent you a present.
Kim - Me?

Donald signals to his general in the back and the man comes forward with the present.
Kim opens it. It's a silk scarf.

Kim (examining the present) - Very nice.
Donald - Hand made. Specially for you. Made in Switzerland.
Kim - Switzerland. Yes. I remember. I go to school there.
Donald - Keep you warm. Bring you good memories.
Kim - Thank you.
Donald - Life in a democracy.
Kim (frowns) - You take risk when you come visit me?
Donald - I do. But I do it because we have to solve this problem we have.
Kim - Yes.
Donald - Kim… I think you're lonely… maybe even depressed…
Kim - I not depressed.
Donald - Sometimes a person can be depressed and not even know it. And it can affect our judgment. Hemingway, one of our great writers, he committed suicide.
Kim - I read this writer. Very good. How he commit suicide?
Donald - With a gun. If he had got help… mental health… he would've worked things out.
Kim - I not depressed.

Donald (to himself) - Hmm… I wonder if the NRA would open a Mental Health division for its membership?
Kim - What?
Donald - Never mind, just thinking aloud. Where were we?
Kim - I not depressed like Hemingway.
Donald - Okay, maybe not. A little paranoid perhaps?
Kim - Paranoid? No.
Donald - Well, don't just dismiss it, consider it as a possibility.
Kim - You say you give me all your 'fire and fury'. I have to protect myself. That not paranoia.
Donald - Kim… I apologize. I was acting crazy.
Kim - How I know when you not act crazy?
Donald - Good question.
Kim - You don't tell me?
Donald (grins) - I like to keep it a secret.
Kim (smiles) - Me too.
Donald - But I'll share something with you, very personal, just because I want us to be open with each other. Part of the reason I came here was to impress the world. Nobody is expecting me to be this bold. The polls show I'm not popular with most Americans. But if we come to some agreement, then, when people find out, there will be great praise for the two of us.
Kim - Me and you?
Donald - Sure. You and me working for the world…. and the world will be happy.
Kim - I like that.
Donald - But if you and I don't reach an agreement and go to war, the world will be sad. Someone will lose more than the other, but no one will win.

Kim looks off.

Donald - How can anyone win when there will be so many

losses? Maybe you'll wipe out San Francisco, or Seoul, or a city or two in Japan... but you know that America will wipe out your country... crush it... I mean, everything. North Korea will be gone. We will give it another name. No more North Korea on the map. Scorched.

(Donald pauses briefly)

And just before you die, the ghosts of your father and your grandfather will come to you and say, 'Kim, what happened? All that effort we put into building the nation, you threw it away?'.

Kim nods pensively.

Donald - There will be no winners, only losers. Would you agree?

Kim - Yes.

Donald - That's great.

Kim - What great?

Donald - What you just said. That simple 'yes', tells me you're not crazy. And because neither you nor I are crazy... we can bond.

Kim - Bond?

Donald - Yeah, bond... get closer to each other. When that happens... then friendship can happen. And you can pick up the phone and call me in the White House, whenever you want. Remember the time difference, though, I like to get my sleep. So you could call me and tell me what's on your mind. And if you're pissed, well, you could tell me that, too. And I would do the same. And we'll respect our differences. That's what John Kennedy did during the Cuban missile crisis in 1962, he picked up the phone and talked to Nikita Khrushchev... and they solved the problem.

Kim folds his arms.

Donald - See… I think you and I could be friends… and I know you would like to have friends in the world community… instead of being so isolated.

Kim nods.

Donald - You'd be able to call up Angela Merkel and shoot the bull with her… or with Teresa May… or Macron… Narendra…
Kim - Shoot bull?
Donald - It has nothing to do with shooting, it's another expression to say you talk about anything, nothing important, just this and that.
Kim - You send me American teacher, yes?
Donald - I told you I would. I keep my promises. Guaranteed. I said I would pass the tax cut and I did.
Kim - Good for hotels?
Donald - Of course, got to take care of number one. But getting back to my point, I'm convinced, that you, Kim Jong-un, supreme boss of North Korea…

Kim sits up in his chair, proudly.

Donald - … would like to have friends in the rest of the world. Just like I have. They love me in India, did you know?
Kim (a hint of envy) - They do?
Donald - Yep. Me and Narendra are tight.
Kim - I know this expression.
Donald - We're selling a lot there, too, the Trump brand.
Kim - Your son take care of business?
Donald - Of course. And he flies in with a secret service detail.
Kim - You smart.
Donald - Thank you. That's what the voters wanted… a businessman… and they got one.

Kim (nods absently) - You feel lonely sometime?
Donald - I do. It comes with having power, but you get used to it. Kim... you want to be recognized as a leader. Just like I do.
Kim - We similar?
Donald - In a way.
(shifting his weight in his seat, leans in)
If you had been born in America, you would've become a billionaire, like me.
Kim - You think?
Donald - No doubt.
Kim - How you know?
Donald - Because you want to be number one.
Kim (grins) - That is true.
Donald - The problem is that people envy us...
Kim - Envy not good. People need to know their place.
Donald - I agree. So, because they're envious... people think we're not really deserving of the position we have. And they will complain and say that you're not deserving because you inherited the job from your father when you were only 27... and in my case, they'll say I'm not deserving because I have a big mouth... and I insult a lot of people... and I was a little crude with women... and white people love me anyway. So, we have to do what we can to prove ourselves.

Kim slams his fist on the arm of his chair. Donald pulls back, just as the officers in the background all take a step forward.

Kim - I already prove myself. I fire missile!

Donald stares at the ground for an instant, then turns to look at Kim in the eye.

Donald - Kim... I've fired missiles too. I sent like 50 of them

to Syria because they used chemical weapons… but that's not enough. We need to prove we can govern.
Kim - I govern. Everybody do what I say.

Donald looks off, wistfully.

The officers in the background all take a step back.

Donald - Harder in America, everybody has an opinion. And some are very loud. I would love for democrats – the blue states – to approve of me. I would love to see the New York Times write an editorial where they praise me. I had a dream about it the other day, that you and I had come to an agreement and everyone was happy, and the NY Times had this headline saying, "Bold leader takes daring leap."
Kim - You think they do it one day?
Donald - No, it's a pipe dream.
Kim (nods)- Pipe dream.
Donald - But I don't let that stop me. I just keep making stuff up, bringing up new ideas, getting people pissed off. But getting back to our topic… Kim, you want to be recognized by the community of nations, am I correct?

Kim shrugs his shoulders.

Donald - Come on, man, of course you want. But you know what the problem is?
Kim - What?
Donald - You don't have much.
Kim - I don't have much?
Donald - All you have is nuclear weapons. Nuclear weapons at the expense of everything else. But look at your brothers and sisters in South Korea. In a very short time, they have gone from

being a colony of Japan to becoming a first world nation.

Kim frowns.

Donald - Now… let's be honest, aren't you a little envious?

Kim does not reply.

Donald - Just a tiny bit?

Kim gets up and walks off a few paces.

Donald (to himself) - Nobody said this was going to be easy.

Donald rises and crosses to stand at Kim's side.

Donald - Kim… how can you not be envious?
Kim - North Korea not envious of South Korea!

The officers in the background all take a step forward.

Donald nods to himself, folds his arms.

Donald - Let me put it another way. If your brothers and sisters, just south of the border, right next door, have the brains and drive to accomplish all they have accomplished, why then, you can too. You're the same people.
Kim - We have brains. Korean scientists solve problem. We are nuclear power. We fire rocket, the world stop and listen to North Korea, every time.
Donald - Kim… that's true… but you can't keep that up… because a mistake can happen, man… which is why I'm here.
Kim - You here to play politics. You here to make democrat in

blue state think you a statesman.
Donald - Not just democrats, Kim, but the whole world. I want everyone to think I'm a statesman. And be honest, man, you want that, too.

Kim returns to his seat. Donald looks after him, then follows and sits down also.

Donald - Kim… everything is negotiable.
Kim - Everything?
Donald - That's right. I'm a businessman… very good, too.
Kim - You think you win next election?
Donald - You're going to help me.

Kim stares at Donald.

Donald - When we agree to a good deal.

Kim laughs loudly. Donald smiles.

Kim - Why you think you win?
Donald - The economies of the whole world are growing again. People are putting money in their pockets. They have more confidence.
Kim - Obama do the hard work. New rules for bank, quantitative easing… all take time.
Donald - Sure, but people forget, so I take credit. And then I cut taxes.
Kim - Tax cut mean big deficit, more debt, then come big inflation.
Donald - We'll deal with it, don't worry. Now, South Korea's success tells you, that North Korea can have the same success. South Korea does not have a nuclear weapon, but they have

accomplished a lot more than you have.

Kim looks at Donald, the expression surly.

Donald - Because they weren't paranoid… they could invest all their effort in the economy.

Kim looks at the ground for a moment.

Donald - I'm trying to be real. Kim… to accomplish as much as they have, you have to change a little.
Kim - Change not easy. I want to stay in power, like father, like grandfather.
Donald - I got that. And I understand.
Kim - You do?
Donald - Yes. In America we have an expression for that… you want to stay 'top dog'.
Kim (laughs) - I know this expression. Me, I stay top dog.
Donald - Yes.

Kim extends his hand to Donald and they shake.
The officers in the background smile at each other.

Donald - Kim, most people in the world will say, 'Kim is a despot… he is a tyrant… he is oppressing his people… starving it… he has to be brought down.' Me, I think differently. I say, you're in transition
Kim - Transition?
Donald - Yes. You're consolidating power. You just took over from your father in 2011. It takes time. But I know you want the best for your people.
Kim - You know this?
Donald - Yes. Without a doubt.

Kim - You smart.
Donald - Thank you. So I say, I will accept you just as you are… and we go from there.

Kim, a bit surprised, is intrigued by the direction the conversation is taking.

Donald - I'm a great believer in the power of personal relationships. That's why I'm here, because I have faith that we can work something out.
Kim - Thank you.
Donald - When we tell the world that there is no longer a threat of a nuclear war, the world will dance in the streets. And I will invite you to come over to the United States.
Kim - What?
Donald - Yes… as my personal guest… to stay with me for a few days at Mar a Lago, my Palm Beach resort.
Kim (smiles) - We play golf?
Donald - Of course. The room rates begin at $ 800 per night. The spa and golf course are extra.

Kim frowns.

Donald - Just kidding.

They share a laugh.

Kim - Very nice of you. Thank you. I think about it.
Donald - Think about it?
Kim (leaning in) - Some people… inside my government… I need to keep an eye on.
Donald - Ah, yes. Same with me. We can never take anything for granted, can we?

Kim - No.
Donald - It's lonely at the top, believe me, I know.
Kim - Very lonely.
Donald - Sometimes it's hard to listen to others. Hard to trust.
Kim - I know this problem. I worry, then I eat too much.
Donald - Same thing here. We're both overweight. (leaning in closer to Kim) You worry, that if you're out of the country, you may not be able to come back?
Kim (leans in a little) - I keep control.
Donald (leaning in a bit more) - Is that why you got rid of your uncle, Jang Song Thaek?
Kim (pulling away) - Too much information.
Donald (backing off) - Of course, I understand. We all have our internal problems. I have mine.
Kim - You have lot of people want to bring you down. Why you not get rid of them?
Donald - It's different in America. Rules, too many rules. I complain… but it's a good system. The people can elect new leaders.
Kim - No elections in North Korea.
Donald - You're not ready for it. The country is evolving… in transition.
Kim (shakes his head) - We different.
Donald - I understand. The main thing, Kim… is that you and I are starting to talk. That is wonderful. Tremendous. Just beautiful. Stupendous.
Kim - Thank you.
Donald - And I am very impressed with your hospitality.
Kim (smiling appreciatively) - You build hotel in Pyongyang?
Donald - I'll think about it… but I want you to know this… I want to become a mentor to you.
Kim - Mentor? Guide?

Donald - Exactly. Now, why do I do that? Because I want to set an example to the world. Actually, Melania has been insisting that I take advantage of the power of dialogue, so we can better understand the way the other side thinks. And she's right. It was her idea, I have to give her credit. She said to me, Dee – she calls me Dee – if world leaders took a little time to mentor the head of a developing nation…
Kim (cutting him off, tersely) - I developed, not developing.
Donald - Kim… no, you're not developed. You're developed in nuclear, but that's it. Just compare yourself to South Korea…
Kim (loudly) - We better than South Korea!

The officers in the background take a step forward.

Donald - No! What's the matter with you? Where are your Kias and Hyundais and Samsungs?
Kim - That because your sanctions!
Donald (calmly) - Kim, that's what Fidel Castro kept saying. The sanctions, the embargo, but no, it's the system.
Kim - System produce nuclear weapon that can go to America. That is big.

Donald gets up and walks front. He needs to take a breather. After a moment, he returns to his seat.

Donald - Kim… during the Cuban missile crisis, in 1962, Castro said to Khrushchev, 'fire the missiles into the United States, that way we solve the problem before it gets worse'.
Kim - What?
Donald - That's right.
Kim - Castro crazy.
Donald - Yes, but Khrushchev was not. So Khrushchev said to his cabinet, 'Castro wants to send us all to the grave.' And

he added, 'let's remove the missiles, it was not a good idea'. Remember that these were missiles that were set up in platforms in Cuba, ready to be fired. That's how close we got to a big war.

Kim nods.

Donald - The world might have come to an end. Your world, my world… everybody's world. But Kennedy was a smart man… and Khrushchev was too… and they had good advisers…. and the two men talked. They made deals. Like we need to make a deal.
Kim - I understand. But I don't remove missiles.

Donald looks down at the ground as he pauses.

Donald - Kim… I come prepared to make you a deal. It is something I have thought about… and that, surely, without a doubt, will bring me a lot of criticism. People will be very angry at me… very, very angry… angrier than the Me Too women are. But I think it's the right thing to do.

They look at each other for a moment, the tension mounting.

Donald - Are you ready?
Kim - I ready.
Donald - I am prepared to offer to you… that you keep the missiles and the bombs you have.

Kim stares at Donald in disbelief.

Kim - I keep weapons?
Donald - You can keep your weapons.
Kim (warily) - What you want from me?

Donald - Don't sell the weapons. Keep them to yourself. No more selling nuclear expertise, or any other weapon expertise, including chemical.

Kim lowers his head, wrings his hands.

Kim - Other nations… ready to pay good money. I need to feed my people.
Donald - That's a choice you made.
Kim - My people get angry.
Donald (sternly) - Kim… pay attention to what I'm saying. I'm offering you a great deal… you keep your missiles, your bombs, but you do not sell them. If we find out that you're selling… we will wipe you out. No questions asked. No more talking. I just erase you from the earth. And then we'll take care of the nation that bought the weapons.

They pause as they look front for a moment.

Donald - What did Castro want when he asked Khrushchev to attack the United States?

Kim says nothing.

Donald - He wanted to be a world leader… in a hurry… and he wanted to do it using the power of the Soviet Union, the power of another nation.
Kim - Castro did not build own missiles, but we do.
Donald - Let me finish. Castro never became a world leader. In his dreams he was, but not in reality. Not because the Cuban people are not smart, but because the Cuban economy didn't go anywhere. And it didn't because people didn't have a chance to develop. And if you don't have that, then the economy can't

grow.
Kim - You think, I, like Castro, want to be world leader in a hurry?
Donald - Yes. Having nuclear weapons won't do it. You're not a big nation just because you have nuclear weapons. It's the economy that makes a difference.

Kim gets up and walks front. Donald remains seated.

Donald - Kim… look at China. What is Xi doing different than you are?

Kim says nothing, his back to Donald.

Donald - Trading with the world. And he's still in power. Isn't that amazing? Xi figured out a way to still be a dictator and have a booming economy at the same time. I don't know how long it's going to last, but that's what you have to do to get started.

Kim nods, deep in thought. He then turns to face Donald, who rises and crosses to join him.

Donald (speaking as he walks) - Or you could be more like us, which I would prefer, but then you'd need to have elections. Xi doesn't bother with elections.
Kim - I don't like elections.
Donald - Too bad. They're fun. Kim… I know you let some people in the elite start private businesses…
Kim - I want economy to grow. I send worker outside of country so they work hard, learn and send money back.
Donald - That's smart. Very smart. And you could do even more of it as you join the community of nations. Do you worry that your business elites will become too powerful?

Kim - No. I control.
Donald - Is there a threat to you from inside the military?
Kim - Too much information.
Donald - I understand. Well, okay.... whatever your situation is, after we make a deal, I would like to keep meeting with you... every month... we can take turns... one time I come over, next time you come to Mar a Lago.
Kim - What you teach me?
Donald - I'll have you meet with the best people in my country, so they can tell you how we do things. You just listen and ask questions. And maybe you'll apply some of the things you learn. It's up to you how fast you'd want to go.
Kim - Thank you. Maybe I make deal?
Donald - Maybe you make deal.
Kim - I think about it.
Donald - Everything has risks, of course. You have your internal problems to deal with and I have mine. People in my country will criticize me, tell me I'm weak, that I like dictators. But I think Melania is right, dialogue can open new possibilities. And like I said before, you can still stay a dictator, like Xi and Vladimir, and El Sisi in Egypt and the Arab princes, and Duterte in the Philippines. But you'll be getting some fresh air.
Kim - Fresh air?
Donald (nods as he taps his temple) - In the brain.

Kim smiles.

Donald - Meanwhile, if you keep your weapons to yourself and don't sell them, I promise you and give you my word of honor, that we, the United States of America will not invade you, unless we think you're getting ready to fire at us, in which case we'll launch a preemptive strike. But I give you my word, that there will be no preventive strike.

Kim looks off.

Donald - And now and then, when you come to Mar a Lago, I'll have a surprise for you.
Kim - What surprise?
Donald - Another world leader will be there and we'll all have dinner together. Play golf too.
Kim - What about sanctions?
Donald - Those will have to wait.
Kim - Why wait?
Donald - Because I have to be sure you're not playing games.
Kim - I don't play game.
Donald - If you're going to test a missile, you'll need to tell us in advance. What kind of weapon and where you're pointing it. We need to know that. This is very important because we don't want mistakes to happen. And I need to be sure you're not sending missiles to another nation. Or plutonium. Or chemical weapons. But as we get to know each other, and you get to know world leaders and you begin to build your economy, then sanctions will be lifted. One at a time.
Kim - You build hotel?
Donald - When you begin to make changes, people will come to visit and I will build hotel. I promise.

They pause. Kim joins his hands under his chin for a moment.

Kim - America in South Korea, that a threat.
Donald - It is not. We're there for defensive purposes only.
Kim - You a threat to me.
Donald - That's your paranoia talking.
Kim - I not paranoid.
Donald - Has South Korea ever invaded you?

Kim says nothing.

Donald - You invaded the South in 1950 which led to hundreds of thousands of people being killed. We fought back but we have never been the first to invade you.
South Korea needs us, and we will be there for them. If you are going to keep calling our presence in South Korea a threat, then you'll have to learn to live with it.

Kim is silent.

Kim - What if we remove nuclear weapons?
Donald - You just told me you would never do that.
Kim - I know… I open to possibilities… what if… North Korea remove nuclear weapons… will you leave South Korea?
Donald - No.
Kim - Why not?
Donald - Because your country has a history of cheating.
Kim - If we allow you inspect nuclear weapons… make sure they gone?
Donald - You would hide them… hide enough of them… and then threaten South Korea so you could take over.
Kim - You don't believe anything I say.
Donald - It will take time to build trust. Baby steps.
Kim - Little by little.
Donald - Yes.

Kim rubs his face.

Donald - Kim, I'm still puzzled why you haven't met with Xi. After all, he's your main trading partner… and helped you evade sanctions.
Kim - Like I say, better for me to stay home. For now. But my

people impatient.
Donald - My people skeptical.

Kim folds his arms over his chest.

Donald - Do you think that a group in your military is connected with Xi, and may want to replace you?
Kim (shakes head) - China is friend. Xi is friend. One day I invite him. Or he invite me and I accept invitation.
Donald - Has he ever invited you?
Kim - Too much information.

Kim then extends his hand to Donald and they shake.

Kim - Thank you for offer, Donald. We get some dinner now, then we talk another day.
Donald - Deal.
Kim - You good with chopstick?
Donald - Very good.

Kim reaches inside his jacket and pulls out a small package.

Kim (handing it to Donald) - This is present to you and your wife. Because you make effort and take risk to come talk to me.

Donald opens it. It's two sets of gold chopsticks.

Donald - Thank you very much. Very kind.

Donald examines and weighs the chopsticks.

Kim (noticing) - Not bamboo.

They laugh. The 4 officers in the background join in the laughter.

5

Mar-a-Lago. Palm Beach. Florida.

Donald and Melania are seated at a table in their suite. Melania is examining the set of gold chopsticks she holds in her hands.

Melania - They're beautiful.
Donald - We'll have the kitchen prepare something Korean so we can use them.
Melania - Of course. So, how was it?
Donald - I thought he was pretty open with me. I asked some probing questions that he refused to answer but, on the whole, it went well.
Melania - You think you can work with him?
Donald - I think so.
Melania - You need an interpreter?
Donald - No. He got everything. And when he didn't he asked. When I spoke to him, it felt like I was talking to a younger version of myself. And even though we're miles apart in terms of political ideology, I ended up liking the guy. I think he got that.
Melania - That's a good sign. Will there be another meeting?
Donald - It's possible. I offered but... at the very end, he wasn't sure.
Melania - Why?
Donald - He's cautious.
Melania - I hope he changes his mind. So, why do you think he's firing the missiles?
Donald - Staking out his territory... establishing his perimeter... afraid we'll invade him... but that's his paranoia. We would never do that, though. It doesn't make sense. But he uses it to

justify his wanting to be king... for life.
Melania (shakes her head slowly) - What cost... personal ambition.
Donald - He's not crazy.
Melania - You can make that statement with certainty?
Donald - Yes. But he's thin skinned.
Melania - Like you.
Donald - And I have been shooting my mouth. I apologized for calling him Little Rocket Man, which wasn't easy.
Melania - Important concession on your part.
Donald - He apologized for calling me "a mentally deranged US dotard."

Donald picks up his set of chopsticks. Looks them over for a moment.

Donald - He liked your present.
Melania - I'm glad.
Donald - I wonder if he was a lonely kid growing up. That couldn't have been easy, being so far away from home, in a boarding school in Switzerland. That's a long way from Pyongyang.
Melania - You went to boarding school, too. Did you feel lonely sometimes?
Donald - Naw. (thinks about it for an instant) I was close to home. But if I did, I ignored it. I was very athletic, made the varsity team in baseball, soccer and basketball, that kept me busy.
Melania - Small school, right?
Donald - You taking credit away from me?
Melania - Just the facts, dear.

She goes to him and sits on his lap.

Melania - I'm proud of you.
Donald - For what?
Melania - For reaching out to Kim.
Donald - Thank you.

She kisses him.

6

Pyongyang. North Korea. Offices of Kim Jong-un. He's at his desk reading a document when he gets a call on his cell.

Secretary - Supreme Leader, His Excellency Vladimir Putin is on the phone, he would like to speak to you.
Kim - Transfer the call.

The two men speak in French.

Kim - Hello?
Vladimir - Hi. How did the meeting go?
Kim - What meeting?
Vladimir - You and Trump.

Kim takes a moment to reply, wondering how the heck the secret meeting was not secret at all.

Vladimir - You there?
Kim - How did you find out?
Vladimir - Kim, there is nothing Russians don't know or can't **find out.** You need to know what brand of underwear Trump likes, we can find out for you.
Kim - So you already know what we talked about?
Vladimir (laughs) - We wouldn't do that to you.
Kim - Very kind of you.
Vladimir - Kim, be careful with Trump. He wants to undermine you. He'd love to see you stop developing nuclear weapons, but he won't stop doing it himself.
Kim - And neither will you. Aren't you putting a lot of money

into new weapons?
Vladimir - To protect ourselves. Purely defensive.
Kim - Same thing I'm doing.
Vladimir - Right… but the Americans do it because they're power hungry. That's what their society is all about, getting more and more power. But they're sneaky, they do it through companies. Google, Apple, Facebook, Microsoft. They call it free enterprise but there's no free lunch, right? We're happy to use their products but they're getting all this data from us. What's that for if not to control us?
Kim - Isn't that what you're doing, too, with your spying?
Vladimir - Kim, we're doing it to defend ourselves, that's all. Did he say anything about me?
Kim - Too much information.
Vladimir - I'm sorry, I didn't mean to be nosey.
Kim - You're nosey.
Vladimir (**laughs**) **-** Love your sense of humor. You like hockey?
Kim - It's all right.
Vladimir - I was wondering if you'd like me to send you our hockey team, to play some games for you. We're the best in the world as you know.
Kim - I like basketball better.
Vladimir - Sure, that's good too, but to get back to Trump and the Americans, you have them scared. That's wonderful, Kim. Only a leader with your commitment to your people can do what you've done. Building nuclear weapons that can bomb America is a great step forward for your country and for oppressed people everywhere. It tells the Americans that they don't own the world.
Kim - Nobody owns the world.
Vladimir - Exactly. But they're pushy. Now everyone has to learn English. Why? What about learning Russian, or Korean? What's wrong with French?

Kim - English is easier. You want to own the world?
Vladimir - What kind of question is that?
Kim - Just a question.
Vladimir - Of course not. We're happy with what we have. Although, to be perfectly honest, just between us, we'd love to have the Ukraine back, and Turkmenistan, Kazakhstan, we love those Caspian Sea shores. Georgia, of course, and Belarus, and eventually we'd like to move up a bit and invite Finland into our great community of nations. We believe that they would love to join us, if it weren't for their corrupt leadership. The breakup of the Soviet Union was a great mistake. Gorbachev allowed himself to be tricked by the Americans. But I'm talking too much. Wouldn't you want to expand into South Korea?
Kim - That would be very nice.
Vladimir - How tragic what happened to the Korean people, how your grandfather, Kim Il-sung, and then your father, Kim Jong-il, worked so hard, sacrificed so much, to unite the peninsula, and how the power hungry Americans stopped them.
Kim - We Koreans are very grateful to comrade Stalin, for giving weapons to my grandfather so we could invade.
Vladimir - You're welcome.
Kim - And we're grateful to China, comrade Mao Zedong, for all the soldiers he sent us to take back the South. Many lives were lost.
Vladimir - If it hadn't been for that bully Eisenhower, threatening to drop the A bomb if China didn't negotiate a truce, Korea would be one nation today.
Kim - That was my grandfather's dream. And my father's.
Vladimir - Eisenhower wanted to get elected so he made the threat. Now it's the same with Trump. His ratings are dropping so he wants something to bring them up again, so he picks a fight with you thinking he can bully you because you're a little nation.
Kim - We're not little.

Vladimir - I meant land wise. But you're a great nation. We recognize that. I'm sure Xi does too.
Kim - My wish is, one day we become exporter of nuclear weapons.
Vladimir - Exporter?
Kim - Yes. So every nation has nuclear power, and there will be no more little nations in the world.

Silence.

Kim - You there?
Vladimir - Kim… I don't think that's a good idea.
Kim - Why not? You don't want people to be equal?
Vladimir - Of course I do. I love equality. The thing is, it takes time to become equal.
Kim - Why wait? We live in the digital age, everything is fast, no more waiting.
Vladimir - Kim, what I mean is… nations have to develop so they learn to have control. For example, you wouldn't want to give a gun to a child, would you?
Kim - You think little nations are children?
Vladimir - No, of course not. What I meant was that having nuclear weapons requires responsibility, and the leaders of some nations are not mature enough.
Kim - You think I'm mature?
Vladimir - Absolutely. In fact, I think that, even though you're half his age, you're more mature than Trump.
Kim - Thank you.
Vladimir - You're welcome. How do I know that?
Kim - How?
Vladimir - You don't tweet compulsively.
Kim - True.
Vladimir - You can hold back on your emotions and reflect on

them.

Kim - Thank you.

Vladimir - But to return to the exporting of nuclear weapons. I'm sorry that we haven't been talking lately but... I must be blunt with you. Kim... please listen... Russia will not accept your exporting nuclear weapons.

Kim - I will do what I want to do.

Vladimir - Kim... not to take anything away from you but Mother Russia did help you build the weapons... we gave you valuable information... rocket designs... scientists... technicians...

Kim - You wanted me to develop nuclear weapons so I could threaten America...

Vladimir - So you could defend yourself... and, of course... the more weapons pointed in their direction the better for us... but we never expected you to be selling them.

Kim - Nobody tells me what to do.

Vladimir (**furious**) - You're being a child! A mad, crazy child! Worse than Trump. Did the Swiss not teach you anything when you went to boarding school there?

Kim is silent.

Vladimir (**taking a breath, calming down**) - Kim, I admire you, really do. The way you have been able to evade sanctions and build your weapons. We helped you with that, too... but it was you who put the work in... your people who suffered deprivation... and then you surprised everybody. That is fantastic. But you're dead wrong about exporting the weapons. Russia will not accept it because we will not know where those weapons go. Do you understand? Kim... Russia has enemies. We will not allow some crazy terrorist coming into our country with a nuclear warhead in his backpack or suitcase, do you understand what I'm saying?

Kim says nothing.

Vladimir - If you sell the weapons to another country, that is exactly what will happen. And I will not accept that. One thing is for you to scare the Americans with all the talk of bombing an American city… that is great… I love to see Americans running scared and putting more money into their military… but when you talk about exporting weapons you have crossed the line. I do not know what Xi has said to you about that, or if he even knows. But I am very clear about it.

Kim is silent.

Vladimir - Are you there?
Kim - I am here.
Vladimir - Kim… if you talk of exporting anything nuclear, I will go over to America' side. You can forget everything I've said about America, I will join with them against you. Do you understand? I don't care what history you and I have together. It will not matter. Talk of exporting nuclear weapons is a no-no. That's it. I will join with the Americans to spy on you and keep the world up to date on where your missiles are and, if we need to… we will destroy you.
Kim - You're very angry.
Vladimir - You do not know what an angry Russian will do. So, be careful.
Kim - I will think about it.
Vladimir - Good. Think hard.
Kim - What if America wants to arm South Korea?
Vladimir - You mean nuclear weapons?
Kim - Yes.

Vladimir - I will not have that. Will not. Did Trump say that to you?
Kim - I said that.
Vladimir - If Trump does that I will accelerate my new weapons development… putting warheads on cruise missiles… missiles that can travel down to the South Pole and up, past their missile defense systems and hit America hard. I'll show him.
Kim - If you do that, America will develop the same missiles.
Vladimir - And I will build more…
Kim - Your economy will go bankrupt, like during the Cold War.
Vladimir - Wait a minute… are you saying their economy is better than ours?
Kim - Yes. The Chinese think so, too.
Vladimir - Really? You thinking of switching sides?
Kim - I will do whatever is good for Kim.
Vladimir - I see. Well… just remember what I said, no exporting nuclear weapons. I'm not fooling around.

Kim says nothing.

Vladimir - Don't want to keep you any longer, just wanted to remind you of who your real friends are.
Kim - Thank you.

Vladimir hangs up.

Kim (to himself) - Putin is as paranoid as I am.

2/7/18
Trump announces that he would like to stage a military parade in Washington.

Trump tweets - In the "old days," when good news was reported, the Stock Market would go up. Today, when good news is reported, the Stock Market goes down. Big Mistake, and we have so much good (great) news about the economy!

He tweets - Best wishes to the Republic of Korea on hosting the @Olympics! What a wonderful opportunity to show everyone that you are a truly GREAT NATION!

He tweets - The Budget Agreement today is so important for our great military. It ends the dangerous sequester and gives Secretary Mattis what he needs to keep America Great. Republicans and Democrats must support our troops and support this Bill!

7

2/8/18

Pyongyang. North Korea. Headquarters of Kim Jong-un. He is seated at his desk smoking a cigarette.

Phone rings.

Secretary (speaking in Korean) - Supreme Leader, your sister wants to speak to you.
Kim - She's on the phone?
Secretary - No, she's here.
Kim - Okay, let her in.

Kim Yo-jong (Little Sister) steps in. She's 30 years old and is wearing a grey pant suit and has her hair done in a ponytail. She strides in confidently and smiling.

Little Sister - Hi big brother.
Kim - Hey, little sister.

She goes up to him and they high five it. Kim returns to sit behind his desk and Little Sister takes a seat opposite him.

Little Sister - How are you?
Kim - Okay. Just got off the phone with Putin.
Little Sister - And?
Kim - Telling me to be careful with Trump.
Little Sister - Hmm. Did you tell him about the secret meeting?
Kim - No.

Little Sister - How did he find out?
Kim - I don't know, but they probably detected the presidential plane on its way here.
Little Sister - You think they have Trump's plane bugged?
Kim - I don't know how they did it but he knew.
Little Sister - Wow.
Kim - I'll check with cybersecurity in a bit… and our espionage division. What's on your mind?
Little Sister - I was thinking… what about if we joined the Me Too movement… in solidarity with American women?

Kim frowns.

Kim - Have you ever been harassed?
Little Sister - When I was in boarding school in Switzerland, a girl tried to get fresh with me and I put her in her place.
Kim - A girl?
Little Sister - A girl.
Kim - I never knew.
Little Sister - I dealt with it.
Kim - You're strong little sister.
Little Sister - Thank you.
Kim - You think some Korean women are harassed by men?
Little Sister - Yep. Just because we're socialists doesn't keep some men from taking advantage of women. It goes deeper than political ideology.

Kim nods pensively.

Little Sister - We could put up a website for women to share their feelings… and we'll get some posters out encouraging them to do so.
Kim - We're worried about the bomb right now.

Little Sister - I'm glad you're bringing that up.

Kim - Trump may order an attack on us.

Little Sister - Kim… do you think that we would be talking about this if Melania were president?

Kim - Melania? She can't be president. She's an immigrant.

Little Sister - I said, if she were president, if she had been born in America and become president. Would we be talking about this?

Kim - I don't know…

Little Sister - We would not, I'm sure.

Kim - You can't be sure.

Little Sister - I am sure, that Melania would not have called you Little Rocket Man. I am very sure of that.

Kim - Hmm.

Little Sister - This whole rocket thing, this is a man thing. Who has the bigger rocket, who has the bigger penis.

Kim (frowning) - Little sister, that is not a way to talk to your big brother.

Little Sister - I am not just your little sister, I am the deputy director of the department of propaganda and agitation, so I need to analyze cultural patterns. That is my job.

Kim - What have you been reading?

Little Sister - Everything… but lately, Freud.

Kim - Sigmund Freud?

Little Sister - Yes.

Kim - That is very decadent, little sister, very decadent.

Little Sister - Why?

Kim - Too much emphasis on the individual instead of the common good.

Little Sister - I have to read everything, so I can better do my job in the department. I have to understand the individual.

They're quiet for a moment.

Little Sister (she stands and starts to pace) - Big brother, I know you have wanted to keep political power and you thought developing nuclear weapons would keep Americans, or anyone else, from interfering. I get that. And I like power very much. I want our family to stay in power, because that's what our grandfather and father wanted for us. And North Koreans should be left alone to decide our fate. But to be firing missiles into the Pacific without giving other nations warning and then talking about hitting America or anyone else, that's crazy.

Kim - Trump started it.

Little Sister - He's got his problems. Macron invited him to Paris on Bastille day and he saw a military parade. Now he orders the Pentagon to plan a military parade of his own. That is not smart. He's being a little kid. It's like, 'You have that? I was impressed. I want it too. I saw yours, now you come see mine'. America does not need a parade. Everyone knows they have the power. Only a very insecure leader would do what he's doing. Did you read what the American press said about it?

Kim - Yes.

Little Sister - So just because Trump started it, doesn't mean you need to get into a bragging match with him. His polls are down. He may not get reelected. Mueller is proceeding with the investigation to see if there was collusion. Trump is scared so he's making a lot of noise. And the stock market took a dive, too.

Kim - I wonder what our polls would say, if we allowed polls?

Little Sister (smiling) - We should leave that alone. I don't see Xi Jinping doing any polls, and their economy is way more advanced than ours.

Kim - Never mind Putin.

Little Sister - That's right. Of course, we could always say it's fake news.

They laugh. Little Sister sits down again.

Little Sister - We did the right thing, to evade sanctions and develop our nuclear weapons. And Americans never thought we had the brains to actually produce the bomb, so now they're surprised.
Kim - Tougher sanctions are not going to stop us.
Little Sister - No. But we should not be answering a threat with another threat.
Kim - That's playing their game.
Little Sister - Exactly.
Kim - You had lunch already?
Little Sister - I had a snack. Thanks.
Kim - I should skip lunch.
Little Sister - Not a bad idea.

Kim laughs.

Kim - I need to eat more veggies.
Little Sister - Stop the sodas. The fried food.
Kim - I'm cutting back.
Little Sister - To get back to that other idea…
Kim - The Me Too movement?
Little Sister - Yes. What do you think?
Kim - Look… I want my daughter to develop as fully as she can… so I do see the benefits of your idea… but let's wait a little.
Little Sister - Okay. But we shouldn't wait too long. The more we let women come into every branch of government, into positions of leadership everywhere, the more balanced and stronger we will be.

Kim nods slowly, not quite enthused by the idea.

Little Sister - When you give your speeches, all the military standing behind you are men, except for me. But there are

women in the crowd, Kim. They need to see that this nation we're building, will offer them - and their daughters - the same opportunities.
Kim - But we must keep the family in power.
Little Sister - I'm all for that. Okay, I must get ready to go to Pyeongchang.

Kim gets up, steps out from behind his desk and flings open his arms. Little Sister goes to him and they embrace.

Kim - Little sister… you will do well at the opening ceremonies. Be graceful and strong.
Little Sister - Thank you, Big Brother. It is an honor to represent you. And I will give your letter to president Moon Rae-in.

She crosses to the exit but turns around before opening the door.

Little Sister - Big brother, I know you won't be the first to fire the missile with the nuclear warhead.
Kim - How do you know that?
Little Sister - I know that… because you love your wife and your daughter, and your older brother and me. But I do worry that a mistake could be made, and then there would be no turning back.

She exits.

Kim remains in his position for a moment, the mood thoughtful, then begins to pace back and forth.

Kim - Little sister has a point. If something went wrong with the rockets I'm firing… it could mean big trouble. Say that there was some glitch with the software… or some bizarre hacker interfered with the instructions while the rocket was in flight… and redirected it to a city in Japan.

Hmmm.

The Americans would retaliate, for sure.

If that happened… I would go all out… fire everything I've got… and then what?

It wouldn't be the end of the world, but we would be wiped out. And maybe South Korea would, too.

And that is not what my grandfather wanted… or my father.

Grandfather wanted a unified Korea. It hasn't happened… not yet.

Father came right after and preserved grandfather's gains, he built us up.

They were not flawless… but those two men were creators. I stand on their shoulders.

Do I want to go down as the destroyer?

I would be remembered as simply that… the impulsive leader who destroyed Korea.

And my daughter would not grow up to be the next leader.

He stops. Smiles.

That would be something, wouldn't it? My daughter, the ruler of North Korea. That, right there, would be a feminist statement. Kind of. But it's going to take some time. History needs time.

He resumes pacing.

Trump is testing me. He has his own problems. He's being the big man, playing to his base. I doubt he'll get reelected… unless, of course, the democrats keep veering left. Anyone can see that America will never be socialist. But if white supremacists keep

coming out of hiding, that will help the democrats.
I'm a bit envious of Americans… their free press… that first amendment thing… I won't tell Trump that, of course, or anyone. If I allowed that here, they'd be tearing me apart… so no… it's not going to happen. Not while I'm alive.
But it's fun to watch them. A big political feast. A wild psychedelic circus.
In a way, if I go by his actions… Trump is a halfhearted believer in democracy… and Americans electing him shows how much anti-democratic sentiment exists in them… which is why they have all that inequality.
Of course, compared to us, it's nothing.
But the fact that Americans are putting it all out there, for the whole world to see, is good for a country. If it can survive it.
Hmm. Maybe not.
It's like they don't care that they live in a glass house.
Is America a good example for the world… even in their madness?
Would I let my daughter go to a boarding school in the West, under an assumed name?
No, of course not. Unless she insists. But it's too far away.
I don't think it's good to be far away from your parents when you're growing up.
Better to bring tutors from America, from France, from China and Russia, so she will learn all four languages. Arabic, too. Five languages altogether. That should be enough. Maybe Spanish too. The education of a leader.

He stops for a moment, then resumes pacing.

I don't doubt that the American model was the inspiration for China's system - the trading part of it. But that model is still evolving. It was Nixon who had the insight to make the move and

reach out to them.
Hmm.
I suppose that Trump is trying to do the same thing with me.
Interesting.
If it hadn't been for the openness of the American system, China would not be where it is today. The Chinese are very smart, no question, but they borrowed and stole from America's intellectual and technological foundation and built on it.
America is not doing it just because they want to be nice. No. For them to get rich, they have to be open. They need new markets. For them to grow strong, they have to trade. It's not an option. Nixon knew that.
When they're open, America exports culture and that's how they conquer the world. That worries me. I don't want their culture to come into mine. Or maybe I do… but then I'd lose control.
Take K Pop, those young South Korean singers and dancers, reworking American songs and coming out with their own style, I love to watch them. Little sister does too.
My older brother, he loves to play American tunes on his guitar. But he was not cut out to be a leader. My father, in all his wisdom, saw that clearly and chose me, instead. I owe the old man.

He stops again.

We're a nation in flux, still evolving, so we need to be left alone. The Japanese had their boots on our throats until the end of World War II. And then we started moving. So that's barely 72 - 73 years. And look how long Americans have struggled with the race issue, and they still can't get it. And the mistake they made bombing Iraq, thinking Saddam had weapons of mass destruction? That was really stupid.
And how about immigration? Ha!

(his expression turns glum)
No one wants to come here. I don't blame them.

He runs his fingers through his hair.

I find him interesting, this Trump fellow. I know so much more about him than he does about me. He was bold to offer to come to see me. But I didn't like that he doesn't want to remove the sanctions. He just flies in and wants to take away my bargaining chip… tells me he will 'let me' have the nuclear weapons. What is that? I have them. Period. He's not 'letting me' anything. I've got them.
But Trump is right that I want to be recognized as a world leader. That's what I've wanted all my life. Ever since my father chose me to succeed him and the servants started calling me Little Prince.
Hmm.
I wonder how much I can get out of Trump. He seems set on his offer.
I need to get him to lift some sanctions.
Our meeting was a good start… but this is my chance to shine on the world stage… my chance to have my name in all the newspapers… to be recognized as a statesman.
Hmm.
Just like he wants.
(now shaking his head) The audacity to compare me with Castro.

8

2/9/18

Trump tweets - Just signed Bill. Our Military will now be stronger than ever before. We love and need our Military and gave them everything – and more. First time this has happened in a long time. Also means JOBS, JOBS, JOBS!

Donald and Melania at the White House, in their suite. Melania is by the window, looking out, Donald is seated at the table, looking at his phone.

Melania - When I go to Seoul, for the conclusion of the Winter Games, I'll get to say hello to Kim Yo-jong, Kim's sister.
Donald - I'm not sure she'll stay for the whole games.
Melania - I'd like to meet her in private.
Donald - What for?
Melania - Just to get to know her.
Donald - I don't know.
Melania - Why not?
Donald - Let the games be the games. Those athletes have been working very hard to be able to compete and they deserve to have all the attention from the press.
Melania - That's thoughtful but… are you perhaps not a bit envious that I would be taking the attention away from you?
Donald - Me?
Melania - Sure, you and Kim having your public feud?
Donald - I am not envious. I even told Kim that I had chosen to meet secretly with him because you wanted me to prove to the world that I was a statesman.

Melania - You told him that?
Donald - Yes, I did.
Melania - And he said?
Donald - He seemed surprised.

Melania crosses to the table and sits next to Donald.

Melania - Dee… let me meet with Kim Yo… I really want to.
Donald - Why?
Melania - Look, she is not only Kim's sister, but she's close to him, and now the youngest member of the Politburo. And the only woman.
Donald - Right.
Melania - So he trusts her and values her opinion. If she and I were to establish a connection, who knows? It might have a bearing in fostering trust between our two nations.
Donald - A feminist connection?
Melania - Beyond that. A connection that might help prevent a war and the loss of life.

Donald is skeptical.

Melania - Why not? Isn't this whole thing about trust?

Donald looks at her.

Melania - Let me help you, Dee.
Donald - And if it flops?
Melania - How could it flop?
Donald - I'm sure she's a pretty tough cookie.
Melania - And I'm not?
Donald - I don't want you to feel awkward… then get irritated and say something wrong.

Melania - Dee, I'm a mature woman, 17 years older than Kim Yo. She could be my daughter.
I'll try to engage her in woman to woman talk. If she doesn't want to engage, then that's that. But what if she wants to? C'mon, mister businessman, what happened to risk taking?

She gets up and returns to the window.

Donald - What will you talk about?
Melania - The importance of having women in positions of power.

Donald frowns.

Melania - Before her, their aunt was the only woman who had been part of the Politburo, but then she was removed when Kim executed her husband in 2013.
Donald - Kim doesn't fool around, does he?
Melania - No, he doesn't.

Donald stares at the floor for a moment, then gets up and joins her at the window.

Donald - Melania… since Koreans have been calling Kim's sister the 'Korean Ivanka'… doesn't it make more sense that I send Ivanka instead?
Melania (pausing for an instant) - I like it. I think it's a better idea. I wish I could go, too, but you're right. They're closer in age.
Donald - Thank you, dear.
Melania - No, you're right. The 'charm offensive' as they call it. I'm sure I'll meet her one day. She made a good impression on me. I think she has a sense of humor.

Donald - Deputy director of the department of Propaganda and Agitation. That's the post she holds. I wonder how humor plays out in that post… but I tell you one thing, if I'd been born in North Korea, that's the department I would've wanted to be part of.
Melania - In charge of fake news.
Donald - You got it. Keep everybody in line.

They laugh.

Melania - We wouldn't have met.
Donald - I'm sure there would have been a hot North Korean gal with your temperament.
Melania - I'm unique.
Donald (caressing her face) - You are.

They embrace for a moment.

Donald - Do you think that my offer to let him have the nuclear weapons makes sense?
Melania - I do. He has the weapons already. The emphasis on bringing him into the world community makes sense. Something like socializing him.
Donald - I'm sure I'll have plenty of critics.
Melania - That you will. Shinzo Abe may not like it.

He ponders.

Donald - Speaking of socializing… the Me Too movement…
Melania - Yes…?
Donald - It's about socializing us guys...
Melania - Yes.
Donald - Learning to respect women…

Melania - Not to take advantage of your position… respecting a woman's voice… seeing them as your equals.
Donald - It's been hard for me.
Melania - It has.
Donald - I have taken advantage of a lot of people…
Melania - The stories keep coming…
Donald - And yet you're here with me.
Melania - Yes.
Donald - Why?
Melania - I love you. I don't accept your behavior… but I love you… and still hope to steer you in a better direction. Call me old fashioned but I believe in marriage.
Donald - You haven't given up hope?
Melania - I'm stubborn.
Donald - What do you love in me?
Melania - Your energy… your feistiness… your sense of humor… and I like being part of the excitement in your life… even with all your quirks.
Donald - You think I'm exceedingly inappropriate… or do I represent a certain kind of male?
Melania - Both. But lately, we've seen lots of men in positions of power being accused.
Donald - It began with Harvey Weinstein, didn't it?
Melania - Yes.
Donald - I would like to talk to you about it… even if I won't ever come out and publicly apologize for my behavior.
Melania - Why not?
Donald - There would be endless lawsuits… while if I deny every instance, it's their word against mine.
But I would still like to try and make sense of it.
Melania - Why have you felt so entitled to another person's body?
Donald - Good question.

His hand on her shoulder, they turn to stare out into the DC night. After a moment...

Donald - I think I have felt superior to women.

She says nothing.

Donald - Superior... in the sense that my accomplishments entitle me to have the woman I want, when I want her.
Melania - Even without her consent?
Donald - Yes. And I am conscious that I've abused my position. And that it's that abuse that women are reacting to... the sense that their bodies have been violated... and that the violation leaves a scar... and that such scars have lasting consequences... and when will it stop.

Melania nods.

Donald - I have been very abusive... but that doesn't mean I can't function as president.

Melania frowns.

Melania - It has implications.
Donald - What do you mean?
Melania - You have been abusive in language and thought while president.
Donald - I have... you think they're related?
Melania - The one leads to the other.

Donald looks down at the ground for a moment.

Donald - If I had not been abusive to women... I would not

have been abusive in language and thought?
Melania - Right.
Donald - That's worrisome.
Melania - It is.
Donald - I don't remember when it started... the abusive behavior... but I think, looking back, that the seed was there all along, that I had picked it up from the culture in which I grew up... the tacit approval of misbehavior... and then, as I became rich and powerful, I felt I had license to do as I wished. And I could always fix it with money if needed.
Melania - Your belief that you don't need women's permission to behave as you have... it rankles...
Donald - It rankles you?
Melania - Yes. The difference with me, is that being your wife, knowing you as I do, up close, I can attest to your strengths and weaknesses... and I know that your feeling entitled comes from a sense of weakness.
Donald - What do you mean?
Melania - As an ambitious male, you're incessantly trying to make your way in the world... but others stand in your path... both males and females... in endless competition... and sometimes you win and sometimes you lose... and tensions rise in you...
Donald - Win or lose?
Melania - And you use the vulnerable woman to placate your unease... win or lose.
Donald - Wouldn't that apply to all men?
Melania - It may... although, obviously, some learn to contain it. In the case of powerful men, it's easier to be tempted to violate women's spaces... because women are attracted to them... like men to powerful women.
Donald - We're all attracted to power.
Melania - There's that allure.

Donald - You were attracted to my power…?
Melania - I was. But I'm more certain than ever that I have my own.
Donald - I've heard stories of powerful women harassing men.
Melania - Yes… but you'll admit that we still live in a male centric society.
Donald - As that changes, and women gain more power, more women will harass men?
Melania - Probably.
Donald - So how do we deal with the problem?
Melania - Good question. I'd say… teach everyone, early on, to find their own power.
Donald - Have you?
Melania - What do you think?

Donald smiles.

Donald - You and I, we're far apart in age… have you ever thought of having an affair?
Melania - No. But if I ever think of it – you'll be the first to know.

Donald reaches over and kisses her.

Donald - Nothing that I have entitles me to violate another human being… encroach upon her… regardless of how much less she may have.
Melania - Add to it an explanation of why you have behaved as you have… then go on TV and state it publicly… and it will be a breakthrough event.

Donald frowns.

Donald - What do you think that would accomplish?
Melania - You would become a model to other men… as befits your position… and you may help them confront their own abusiveness.
Donald - My base would kill me.
Melania - Dee… you have to stop being afraid of your base. You're now president. The power is yours. Your base elected you but doesn't own you. You have to do what is right, what you think is best for the entire nation. Not what is best for a faction or group.

You have to be president to all Americans… and if you don't get elected a second time, well, then you don't. But you will have exercised your power in the best interest of the nation. And that is something that would be a mark of enduring distinction. One great term as president is much better than two mediocre ones.
Donald - Sweetheart, I don't know if you have found your power or not, but you have certainly found your tongue, because you can surely wag it good.

She laughs.

Donald - I wish… in hindsight… that women would've been more forceful when I mistreated them.
Melania - Slapped you in the face?
Donald - Yes. Or simply told me off, forcefully.
Melania - That would've stopped you?
Donald - Yes.
Melania - They call that blaming the victim.

He looks out the window, deep in thought.

Melania - Some women can set limits. Others are intimidated. And we all need to learn how to do that. But centuries of being treated as a second-class person doesn't vanish overnight. There are the invisible scars… like with racism. Still, whether a woman can or cannot stand up for herself and set boundaries, the problem starts with you, you as the transgressor.

He nods slowly.

Donald - Would you like to have a glass of cider?
Melania - Yes.

They cross to the table. Donald goes into a nearby closet and gets the bottle and glasses.
He sets them on the table and opens the bottle. They sit at table. She pours from the bottle.

Melania - The gifts that you have, while enabling you to rise to this position, have made your flaws more glaring… but there is much that you can do to remedy them… and in so doing learn to govern better.
Donald - Intemperance in one realm can easily seep into another… to everyone's peril.

He raises his glass to offer a toast.

Donald - To us.
Melania - To us.

They clink and sip.

Donald - In theory, if I began to act to address my core intemperances… I might be able to alter some perspectives I now have.
Melania - You might.

Donald - But… isn't it too late for that sort of thing?
Melania - Not at all.
Donald - You have faith in me?
Melania - Still do.

They sip again.

Donald - I do worry that changes I make may end up alienating my followers.
Melania - In the end, it is not others' approval that matters the most…
Donald - … but that that you give yourself. That may be true for some folks, but politicians tie their fortunes to peoples' approval.

He puts his glass down and reaches for her hand and pulls her to him, sitting her in his lap. He looks at her, caresses her hair.

Donald - I love you. Thank you for sticking with me.

She returns the caresses.

Donald - Sweetheart… in the privacy of our bedroom… I'd like to remain a brute… if you don't mind.

She smiles mischievously.

Donald - It gives me a great deal of pleasure.
Melania - I understand.
Donald - What does that mean?
Melania (winking at him) - I can work with it.
Donald (nodding appreciatively) - Who's given you the most pleasure, ever?

Melania (resting her head on his shoulder, enjoying the moment) - You have.
Donald - Admit it, you love your brute.
Melania (into his ear, whispered lovingly) - Not just love... I adore my brute.

They kiss.

Donald - You want me to show you who's boss?
Melania - You're not too tired?
Donald - For some things... I'm never tired.

They stand and he leads her to their bed but she stops him, looks him in the eye.

Donald - What?
Melania - Sing something to me...

He looks at her tenderly... then takes her hand in his and asks...

Donald - My beautiful lady... would you care to dance?
Melania - I would.

He circles her waist with his arm and draws her to him... leading her in dance... moving slowly toward the window... while he sings...

Donald - Love... is a many splendored thing...

... and they sway in each other's arms in the moonlight... and then kiss.

He then sweeps her off her feet and carries her to bed. She turns the lights off.

After a long and sweet moment, Melania turns the lights back on. They are lying next to each other.

Melania - You were so gentle.
Donald (smiling triumphantly) - I knew I could do it.

She kisses him on the cheek.

Melania (suddenly remembering) - Oh, my god, we're going to miss the opening ceremonies!

They sit up and turn on the TV. A moment later the announcer says that the combined team of North and South Korea is about to enter the stadium.

Melania - Wow, look at them.
Donald - Yep.
Melania - There they are!

As the parade of beaming athletes stream in, the crowd in the stadium waves and cheers. Then the camera pans to the area where Mike Pence and his wife are seated, their expressions solemn. Behind them, standing proudly, are Kim Yo-jong, Kim's little sister, and the President of North Korea, Kim Yong-nam.

Melania - Wait a minute, why aren't Pence and his wife standing?
Donald - I don't know. In protest I suppose.
Melania - But… that doesn't make sense, there are North and South Koreans athletes marching together. Common courtesy would have it that you should stand.

Donald - I'm sure Mike thinks he's doing the right thing.
Melania - You didn't tell him not to stand, did you?
Donald - No.
Melania - They probably haven't talked either. Did you ask them not to talk to the North Korean delegation?
Donald - Not at all.
Melania - I don't like that. Makes us look boorish.
Donald - You're right. Honey, next time, I'll send you instead.

2/10/18

Seoul.

At the presidential Blue House, Kim Yo-jong, meets with South Korea's President, Moon Jae-in, and extends an invitation from her brother, Kim Jong-un, to meet in Pyongyang. President Moon expresses interest in the proposal, adding that he would like for North Korea to also enter into talks with the US.

Vice president Pence responds by stating that Kim Jong-un must first dismantle "permanently and irreversibly" nuclear and ballistic missiles before any negotiating over sanctions reductions can begin.

South Korean analysts reply that it would not be wise for South Korea to reject the North's offer, since it is South Korea that would suffer the most if a weapons miscalculation were to occur.

Other commentators said that the offer for the two nations to meet represented another effort from the North Korean leader to have sanctions eased on his nation without making concessions of his own, and was aimed at putting some distance between the US and South Korea.

President Moon Rae-in has previously expressed the opinion that he is open to talks so long as they would be contributing to the resolution of the weapons crisis.

Joint military exercises between the US and South Korea scheduled for February have been pushed back in deference to the Winter Olympics and Paralympics in Pyeongchang.

Shinzo Abe, the Japanese leader, upon hearing of the offer from Kim Jong-un, said to president Moon that he should hold the joint military exercises right after the Olympic games and not wait any longer. President Moon told him to mind his own business.

Xi Jinping, the Chinese leader, stated that the US could stop their military exercises with South Korea in return for the North suspending their nuclear weapons program.

But a spokesperson for the North Korean leader stated emphatically that his nation will not give up its nuclear weapons.

In a sudden reversal of position, vice president Pence said that the US would be willing to talk to North Korea without any preconditions. Wags have commented that Mr Trump must have called Pence and told him to simmer down.

9

2/11/18

Pyongyang. North Korea.

Kim Jong-un is at his desk in his office. His secretary calls him on the phone.

Secretary - Supreme leader, the President of the United States wishes to speak to you.
Kim - Transfer the call.
Donald - Kim, how are you?
Kim - I am well.
Donald - Cold up there?
Kim - Very cold.
Donald - Cold here, too. Heard the news about your wanting to meet with president Moon Rae in. I think it's great.
Kim - You do?
Donald - Yes. This is a milestone. First time you meet with a foreign leader… I mean, publicly. Terrific. When do you think it'll happen?
Kim - Not sure.
Donald - You don't want to lose the momentum.
Kim - No. You tell him about our secret meeting?
Donald - No. That's between you and me. When the time comes, we'll make the announcement together. We'll tell the world that we had met privately before all of this happened.
Kim - Good. So what you say to Moon now?
Donald - Moon is his own man… but I will suggest that there should be no monetary concessions. But he knows. I've heard

him say that they don't want to make the mistakes of the past. Neither do we.

Kim is quiet.

Donald - Kim?
Kim - How I feed my people?
Donald - If you didn't put all that money into building weapons you could be feeding your people. This can be over today if you wanted. You know my position. Do the right thing and I will respect your boundaries. No invasion.
Kim - What about sanctions?
Donald - I need to see that you're serious and we will lift them slowly. If you start coming to Mar-a-Lago, I'll introduce you to world leaders, business leaders too, to help your economy grow… and so you don't feel so isolated.
Kim - Maybe President Moon make better deal. South Korea independent nation.
Donald - Kim… let's not play games.
Kim - No games.
Donald - You are playing games. I have made a big concession to you, huge - you can have the weapons - but no exporting them. You can make a decision right now and we will stun the world.

Kim says nothing

Donald - Do we have a deal?
Kim - Have to think about it.

Donald shakes his head, grumbling.

Donald - You piss me off, you know that?

Kim - I know that expression.
Donald - Good. Because here I am, putting myself out, making an effort, maybe even get creamed by my base, and you're blowing me off.
Kim - You don't have to eliminate people, like I do.
Donald - You could put them in jail, instead, couldn't you?
Kim - They can still plot from jail. To be safe, better eliminate. No more plotting.
Donald - That's bad business, Kim. I've never eliminated anyone but, there was a time when I thought that playing rough was necessary. Like when I was in favor of waterboarding… you know, torturing terrorists. I've changed my mind.
Kim - Why?
Donald - I've talked to people about it. Jim Mattis, in the Defense Department. He told me he'd get as much information from a terrorist just by sitting down and having a beer with him.
Kim - You believe that?
Donald - I do.
Kim - Donald, I have bridge in New York I want to sell to you.
Donald - Not funny. The point is to talk, man. That's why I've reached out to you. This could be the beginning of you joining the world community.
Kim - We different.
Donald - No you're not. Except for the paranoia.
Kim - I not paranoid. I tell you what help me.
Donald - What?
Kim - You announce you have no more military exercise with south Korea, not just postpone.
Donald - Why?
Kim - That way I look stronger… and I have more time to find people who plot against me and eliminate them.
Donald - That's a story you're telling me, Kim. Nothing more. No military exercises means you getting more ships in with goods

and fuel to bypass the sanctions. Anyway, I checked with the CIA, they assure me there's no one plotting against you.
Kim - Donald, I know more about North Korea than CIA, okay?

They pause.

Donald - These people you say are plotting against you, are they pro-Russian or pro-Chinese?
Kim - Don't know.
Donald - Okay, then I don't know either. So, we will continue the military exercises until you join the world community. South Korea can do nothing about that. If they want to join, fine, if not, then we do the exercises ourselves.
Kim - Then I ask president Moon for help with food and fuel.
Donald - They will not do that. The money going into bombs, use it to grow food.
Kim - South Koreans are our brothers.
Donald - Right, and they have not forgotten what your leaders have done… that your father blew up that passenger plane in '87 and killed 115 people, that in 2010 he torpedoed one of South Korea's ships and killed 46 sailors, that your grandfather invaded them in 1950 which cost hundreds of thousands of lives… hundreds of thousands of your brothers… killed because your grandfather thought it was a good idea to take over South Korea.

Kim says nothing.

Donald - So the sanctions stay… the United Nations imposed them. South Korea obeys the sanctions because it is part of the world community, while you are not.
Kim - I try anyway.
Donald (exasperated) - You know what I'm going to have

to do? Proceed with my plan to put nuclear weapons in South Korea.
Kim - Not good idea. China say no to that.
Donald - Too bad. It is San Francisco you want to bomb, not Beijing. They should've stopped sending you oil a long time ago.
Kim - Talk to Xi first.
Donald (ignoring him) - In the meantime, I'm going to call world leaders, so we can set up a surveillance system, to monitor the traffic of nuclear weapons. You remember the blockade of Cuba during the missile crisis in 1962?
Kim - I read about it.
Donald - I cannot take chances with you exporting nuclear weapons. And one way to do that is to set up a blockade.
Kim - Not good for me and internal problem. I talk to Moon, he put pressure on you to prevent that and to stop military exercise indefinitely.
Donald - Remember what I said, you can join the world community the moment you make a commitment to peace. And that means not exporting nuclear weapons. If you do, I can even ask the CIA to help you solve your internal problem.
Kim - Not good idea.
Donald - They have experience with waterboarding… no, scratch that… it was just a slip, sorry.

They pause.

Kim - You send Ivanka to closing ceremonies?
Donald - Ivanka? Hmm. Maybe.
Kim - You compete with North Korea, see who more charming, my sister or your daughter.
Donald - They're both pretty charming.
Kim - Maybe they can meet?
Donald - Sure, that sounds good. Think about the offer I

made… it's on the table now, but I may remove it later.
Kim - You play games.
Donald - Think, Kim. Think. Mar-a-Lago would be good for you.
Kim - I think.

Donald hangs up.

10

2/12/18

Beijing. Offices of Xi Jinping.

Xi is seated at his desk shuffling some papers
His secretary rings him on his phone.

Secretary - Supreme Highness, Trump is on the phone. Should I put him on hold for a while or do you want to speak to him?
Xi - It's okay, I'm taking a break, I'll talk to him. Transfer the call.
Donald - Xi, man, how are you?
Xi - Hi, Donald, how have you been?
Donald - Cold over there?
Xi - Very. How about you?
Donald - Cold but I don't mind. I can always hop over to Mar-a-Lago, play a little golf. Tax payers are going to kill me when they see the bill, but heck, a president has to be comfortable. How's your main squeeze?
Xi - My what?
Donald - Slang for wife. Friendly thing.
Xi (after a pause, soberly) - She's fine. Thank you. How about your squeeze?
Donald - Oh, man, great, really great, hottest chick I've ever had. So, Xi, when are you coming over again?
Xi - Let's plan it.
Donald - Be glad to have you. Xi… about the military exercises with South Korea… we can't postpone them indefinitely.
Xi - I said to postpone them while he halts his nuclear program,

that's all. I think he's having some domestic problems...

Donald - I don't believe it. My spies tell me there's nothing to that. After he cleaned house in 2013 and eliminated his aunt's husband, nobody has dared to say anything against him. Of course, people keep defecting.

Xi - Well, Donald, your spies may be better than mine but I'm hearing a different story.

Donald - What do you think is going to happen when Kim and Moon talk?

Xi - Nothing will happen. You hold the pieces. They'll end up talking about hockey.

Donald - You think Moon will pull out of the military exercises, if Kim asks him?

Xi - Of course not, plus his opposition won't let him. But Kim will ask for help because the situation at home is difficult. Not everybody eats, as you know. We've tried our best to give assistance, for humanitarian reasons. He needs to shift to food production instead of bombs.

Donald - Xi... I cannot have Kim threatening to fire a missile to the West Coast. Even though they're mostly democrats.

Xi - What?

Donald - Just kidding. I'm very serious about this.

Xi - We're cooperating with the sanctions, Donald, doing all we can.

Donald - Xi... I'm thinking of organizing a naval blockade.

Xi - What?

Donald - A blockade of the entire Korean coast... west and east... so that no nuclear weapon gets out... of course that would mean that you would have to blockade him on land.

Xi - That is madness.

Donald - Why?

Xi - I would not accept having all those American war ships right outside our territorial waters.

Donald - It would be a joint effort of the world community.
Xi - I will veto it in the Security Council. I'm sure Russia will too.
Donald - You have internal problems, also?
Xi - None of your business. A blockade will not happen, so let us be clear about that.
Donald - Then you leave me no option.
Xi - What do you mean?
Donald - I will have to put nuclear weapons in South Korea.
Xi - What? No! Absolutely not!

Silence.

Donald - They will be pointing to North Korea.
Xi - I don't care! Look, the sanctions are working. We need to give it time.
Donald - We've run out of time. Kim will not export nuclear weapons. Whatever he has to do inside North Korea, he has to do, but I have to protect my country.
Xi - I have to do the same.
Donald - Stick to the sanctions.
Xi - I told you I would.
Donald - I've given orders to monitor any movement of weapons out of North Korea… we have our satellites checking every inch of their coast… if we see anything that looks remotely like a missile it will be stopped, United Nations or not. So, if any weapon does get out it will be through the border with China.
Xi - Nothing will get out.
Donald - Do I have your word?
Xi - You have my word.
Donald - This has gone on long enough.
Xi - Yes.
Donald - Well, let me know when you want to come back to

Mar-a-Lago. Play a round of golf. Say hello to your lady.
Xi - I will. Hello to Melania.

11

2/12/18

Pyongyang. North Korea.

Kim Jong-un in his office with his sister, Kim Yo-jong. They sit across each other, a small coffee table in between. Kim Yo-jong has just returned from the Winter Olympics in Pyeongchang, where she represented her brother.

Little Sister - It was a wonderful trip. South Koreans were very nice to me. And you saw how everybody applauded when the athletes marched in under one flag. It was very exciting. I wish you would've been there.
We're one people, Kim.
Kim - That's what grandpa used to say.
Little Sister - President Moon and his wife, very nice, too.
Kim - You think he will come?
Little Sister - Yes. I think they expect some movement on the nuclear weapons issue.
Kim - Yes, of course.
Little Sister - I know you've said that we will continue with our nuclear weapons program...

Kim nods thoughtfully.

Kim - We can't go back on that. That's what grandfather and father wanted.
Little Sister - I know.

She lowers her head.

Kim - What do you think?
Little Sister - Things change… I mean… it's not like we're Pakistan and they have a history with India and India has nuclear weapons and they're next to each other and Pakistan had to develop their own. Our situation is different.
Kim - How so?
Little Sister - Well, China is our friend… and South Korea wouldn't invade us… any more than West Germany would've invaded East Germany. Plus the South doesn't have nuclear weapons.
Kim - And?
Little Sister - Americans wouldn't invade us, either. If they had a crazy leader, maybe. But Trump isn't crazy. He's insecure and likes to brag, but he's not crazy. The only way America would feel they had a green light to invade us would be if we started the hostilities.

Kim gets up and walks a few paces. There are no windows in his office, which is in a heavily fortified underground area.

Kim - You think the nuclear weapons program is not a good idea?
Little Sister - I thought it was… but I'm having my doubts. I mean, I still would like the family to stay in power but… this is a new world… different than grandpa's and our father's… and we should start working toward reunification.

Kim nods slowly as he clasps his hands.

Kim - Reunification would mean only one system, little sister… only one… which will it be?

Theirs or ours?
Little Sister - I would want our family to stay in power.
Kim - Little sister, answer my question, theirs or ours?
Little Sister - Big brother… I love you dearly… and I would do anything for you… but people there seemed happier than ours.
Kim (brusquely) - That's because of the sanctions! If we didn't have them we could be doing what China is doing.
Little Sister - Then give up the nuclear program.
Kim - Give it up? Did you just say that?
Little Sister (lowering her head, contritely) - Yes, I did.
Kim (a note of sadness) - Little sister…
Little Sister - Or maybe we could keep the nuclear program going but go more slowly, so we could have more money for food and to develop the economy. We're a smart people, Kim. We could have as much wealth as South Koreans have. Maybe even more. We could be inventing and exporting things, and people would be coming to see what we're doing. We could be an inspiration to other peoples.
Kim - What would happen to me?

They're quiet for a moment.

Little Sister - We do it slowly… all the while keeping a firm hand on the military… like Xi is doing… I'm sure he'll be there forever. And when he gives it up, if he ever does, the party will be there to protect him.
Kim (skeptical) - You really think we could transition to something like the Chinese model?
Little Sister - Yes!
Kim - What about the people I've had to eliminate, little sister? What about their ghosts?
Little Sister - What about Mao's ghosts, all those people he eliminated during the time he was in power? Or Xi's ghosts? Or

Putin's? I'm sure they're around. But if you have a strong party, the ghosts will not take away your power.
It can be done.

Kim gives a long look at his little sister.

Kim - Little sister, you have spoken from your heart and I appreciate it. For now, however, you will be suspended from your position as deputy director of the department of propaganda and agitation. You will be confined to your home but you will not lack anything you desire.
You understand?

Little Sister (lowering her head) - Yes, big brother.
Kim - Come, give me a hug.

Little Sister gets up and gives her brother a hug.

Kim - I will call you soon.

Little Sister bows and exits.

Kim starts to slowly pace up and down his large office.

Kim - All that she said makes sense. My country and China have been next to each other all this time, and yet, our development has been so different. And I can say the same thing about South Korea.
For one reason or another, my country has fallen behind.
I have known that and I do not like it.
I cannot stand here and say that I am more virtuous than my neighbors. I have no grounds to say that.
I can say, that my country has not been open.

We have been very secretive… and have isolated ourselves.
It's not all about the sanctions.

He stops.

This is not easy for me.
I was only 27 years old when I took power after my father's death in 2011. Some would say I was too young. And I may be forgiven some mistakes. But I have not, for one moment, looked back at my ancestors and questioned whether they had taken the right road.
A leader of a country, no matter how young, cannot be blind to his past. I fear now that I have been.
My little sister, instead, seems to have the eyes to see the truth. I fear that I envy her.
As I watched her on television, I saw joy in her heart.
I secretly wished I had been with her.
So what is there for me to do now?
Accept my mistakes? Or keep making new ones?
A transition appears inevitable.

He resumes pacing.

Is it possible that we could have two political systems, side by side? Both with strong and open markets, but one with a democratic system and the other with a system modelled after China's?

He stops again.

I do know, that I will not relinquish power. I will not. And I will not give up my nuclear weapons.
I would like to think that one day soon, we could have

open borders with the South. And maybe that will be how reunification will start. But I will not give up power.

His secretary calls him on the phone.

Secretary - Supreme leader…
Kim - Yes.
Secretary - Mr Trump wishes to speak to you.
Kim - Transfer the call.
Donald - Kim?
Kim - Yes?
Donald - How are you, man?
Kim - I am well, thank you.
Donald - There's a lot going on right now, so I was thinking you and I should meet again.
Kim - That would be fine.
Donald - Very well, then, when?
Kim - I look at schedule and I call you back.
Donald - Okay. I'll be waiting for your call. Thanks.

2/14/18

Parkland, Florida.

A gunman, a former student, entered the Marjory Stoneman Douglas High School and killed 17 students and wounded 17 others.

Trump tweets - My prayers and condolences to the families of the victims of the terrible Florida shooting. No child, teacher or anyone else should ever feel unsafe in an American school.

12

2/16/18

The White House. Morning.

Donald and Melania in their suite. Melania is at the window, Donald is seated at the table, deep in thought.

Robert Mueller has just announced the indictment of Russian citizens and companies for interference in America's 2016 elections.

Melania - So what do you think?
Donald - It has nothing to do with me. Their interference began way before I decided to run.
Melania - But there's no question that they meddled.
Donald - Yes, but no proof that it had a bearing in the election results.

Donald leans forward, arms rested on his thighs and hands joined.

Melania - You still believe Putin had nothing to do with it?
Donald - I don't know anymore.
Melania - The press keeps saying you're soft on him.
Donald - He's innocent until proven guilty. So far, there's no proof of his involvement. The press will always find fault with me. I'm not their darling. But I have a lot on my plate and my own way of doing things.

He looks at her.

Donald - I'm not hiding anything. I did nothing wrong.
Melania - And that meeting in June 2016, with a Russian citizen, in Trump Tower, your son Donald and Jared and Manafort, concerning information the person allegedly had that could be used against Hillary Clinton?
Donald - I had nothing to do with it. Nothing.

Melania crosses to the table and sits next to him.

Melania - Dee… you were the underdog… desperate to pull ahead of the other contenders… maybe not even fully aware of the implications of such a meeting… did you, unwittingly consent to such a meeting? Did your judgment falter at that critical moment?
Donald - No. But that's probably what Mueller will ask me when we meet.

Melania reaches over to cover Donald's hands with her own.

Melania - What do you want from me?
Donald - I want you to believe in me.
Melania - I believe in you.
Donald - Thank you.

He takes her hand to his lips and kisses it.

Donald - The Left has been after me since the beginning… and I have given them ample reason for I have been outlandish and ill-considered… but as I see it, I need to have a working relationship with Putin. The world is too complicated not to have one. But if one day, proof is found of his involvement, then I will react accordingly. And he will have my fire and fury.

Late that evening – from Florida.

Trump tweets - Our entire nation w/one heavy heart, continues to pray for the victims & their families in Parkland, FL. To teachers, law enforcement, first responders and medical professionals who responded so bravely in the face of danger: we THANK YOU for your courage!

13

2/18/18

Trump tweets - I never said Russia did not meddle in the election, I said "it may be Russia, or China or another country or group, or it may be a 400 pound genius sitting in bed and playing with his computer." The Russian "hoax" was that the Trump campaign colluded with Russia – it never did!

He tweets - If it was the GOAL of Russia to create discord, disruption and chaos within the U.S. then, with all the Committee Hearings, Investigations and Party hatred, they have succeeded beyond their wildest dreams. They are laughing their asses off in Moscow. Get smart America!

The White House.
The Oval office. Evening. Donald, Melania and Ivanka are seated by the fireplace.

Donald - It's a great time for you to meet with Kim Yo-jong.
Ivanka - For real?
Donald - Yes. I've been thinking about it.
Ivanka - Dad, I love the idea.

She gets up and crosses to the window, excited at the prospect.

Donald - It would probably mean you going there.
Ivanka - Of course. I'll meet her anywhere.
Donald - We have to keep pushing forward on the reunification idea. Building bridges, right Melania?

Melania (smiles) - That's what it's all about.
Ivanka (covering her face with her hands, a look of astonishment in her eyes, then crossing back to join Donald and Melania) - Dad!
Donald - What?
Ivanka - You know what I just thought? I could tell Kim Yo-jong about my brand… talk about starting a clothing line in their country.
Donald - I love it.
Ivanka - Did you know that President's Moon's son, Moon Joon-yong has a master's from Parsons School of Design in New York?
Donald - Really? I might've bumped into him. How old is he?
Ivanka - About my age. Last I heard he was working as a freelance designer. We could recruit him.
Melania - Moon has a daughter, too.
Ivanka - Yes. Married, has a child, stays out of the limelight. We could bring her in at some point. Get her input for a clothing line for kids.
Donald - Beautiful, just beautiful. Business will bring the world together. In fact… I've been thinking… now that the economy is perking along, I could tell my base that it's time to get back into the Trans Pacific Partnership. They're moving right along without us. I hate to be left out of a good thing.
Ivanka - We could do a very affordable brand.
Donald - Of course. I'd like to meet his sister, too. I'll ask him.

Ivanka is startled.

Ivanka - Dad…?
Donald - What?
Ivanka - You've been talking to Kim?

Donald looks at Melania, back to Ivanka, then smiles slyly.

Donald - Keep it under your hat. No one knows about it.
Ivanka - That's wonderful. Really bold and creative of you.
Donald - Thank you, dear.
Ivanka - I'm proud of you.
Donald - Actually, it was Melania who spurred me on.
Ivanka - Really?
Donald - She said to me, you need to prove to the world that you're a statesman. So I figured, I'd borrow a page from Richard Nixon. He had his famous 'opening to China' moment. I figured I could have my 'opening to Korea' moment.
Ivanka - Dad, that's brilliant.
Donald - Thank you. Don't tell anyone.
Ivanka - Of course not. Who else knows about it?
Donald - Kelly and Mattis.
Ivanka - Not Pence?
Donald - Not yet. I have him on a need to know basis.

Ivanka and Melania exchange a glance.

Donald - He's a fine fellow, I have nothing bad to say about the man, very loyal, but when I run again in 2020, I'll need to pick a woman for VP.
Ivanka - Brilliant! Oh my god, yes! How come I didn't think about it?
Melania - Your dad has his great moments.
Donald - I figure I owe it to the women of this country. And, of course, it would help divide the women vote.
Ivanka - Dad, you're a genius!
Donald - Thank you.
Ivanka - But what about Pence?
Donald - He'll be fine. He'll go back to Indiana. Or, I'll create a cabinet position for him…
Ivanka - What?

Donald - I don't know.
Melania - Secretary of Religious Affairs.
Donald - Thank you, dear.

Donald gets up and saunters over to the window as he talks.

Donald - I figure the Me Too movement will continue to gather steam and a woman VP would be a way of countering it. But I expect the economy to be the deciding factor. With the tax cuts moving us forward, I can only see more and more growth. A little inflation, sure, but the growth will be terrific. And if we run into a little slump, heck, I'll push for another tax cut.
Ivanka - That's great.

Ivanka and Melania rise and join Donald by the window.

Ivanka - Dad… this may appear to be too bold on my part… it just occurred to me… the same way you get your ideas… but at least consider it…
Donald - Okay… out with it.
Ivanka - If you want to go with a woman VP… which is definitely brilliant… why not choose me?

Donald and Melania look at each other.

Donald - Not just one Trump but two? A double Trump. You'd be what… 39 by then?
Ivanka - Yes.
Donald - The youngest VP ever?
Ivanka - No, that was Breckinridge, VP to Buchanan, served only one term, between 1857 and 1861. And I'd be more than ready to run for president after your second term ended.
Donald - Wouldn't that be something, a 16 year run for the

Trumps?
Ivanka - It would be lovely.
Donald - Let alone the possibilities for our brand.

Donald opens his arms wide and brings the two women into a group hug. When they pull back, he walks off, deep in thought. Then he turns around.

Donald (addressing Ivanka) - I'll give it some thought, but it may be premature to go with you. Someone more seasoned might be better… maybe one of the lady senators… or… to further unify the country… a conservative democrat.
Ivanka - Dad! The party will revolt.
Donald - I'll break with tradition and not mention the VP choice until after I'm nominated at the convention. Inject some drama into the proceedings. And then, bang! I'll surprise everybody.
Ivanka - That's madness!
Melania - It's just something he's trying out. He's thinking aloud.
Donald - Thank you, dear.
Ivanka - I will prove to you that I'll be ready for the challenge. You wait and see.
Donald - I do have something I'd like for you to do.
Ivanka - What?
Donald - Would you like to represent me at the closing ceremonies in Pyeongchang?
Ivanka - Yes! Of course!
Donald - Kim Yo Chong will not be there, that we know of. I suppose her brother could always pull a surprise move at the last moment, but we'll announce your trip on the 21st and you'll leave the next day. So go out there and charm everybody.
Ivanka - Thanks, dad. I'll start preparing right away.

She goes to him, gives him a hug and a kiss, does the same with Melania, and exits.

Donald (to Melania) - About being my VP… she may surprise me yet.
Melania - Let's wait and see.

On 2/23/18, Ivanka Trump arrives in Seoul and later that evening has dinner with President Moon Rae-in at the Blue House. She affirms bonds of friendship and the American commitment to "maximum pressure" to bring about the denuclearization of the Korean peninsula.

Hours after the meeting, Trump announces new sanctions. They will target ships from nations known to be trading with North Korea (China, Singapore, Hong Kong, Tanzania, Comoros, the Marshall Islands, Panama, Taiwan). The objective is to stop North Korea's exports of coal and imports of oil as well as illegal ship to ship transfers at sea. The US will ask countries to permit inspections of ships it deems suspicious.
Trump stated, "if sanctions don't work we'll have to go to phase 2… phase 2 may be a very rough thing – may be very, very unfortunate for the world."
An economic blockade of North Korea is being considered but is expected to be opposed by China and Russia.
In December 2017, China said no to a United Nations proposal to board ships in international waters.

2/25/18

News Item - China announces that it will remove the term limits for president and vicepresident. Xi Jinping may then be able to remain president beyond 2023.

14

2/26/18

Pyongyang. North Korea. Kim Jong-un's office.

There's a golf practice set-up lying between the coffee table area and his desk. Kim is working on his putting.
He positions the ball… carefully measures the distance to the hole…
His cell starts to ring.
He ignores it.
He is completely absorbed in the task of hitting the ball with the right force.
The cell continues to ring.
He taps the ball… rolling… rolling… and… it drops in the hole.

Kim (pumping his hand in the air) - Yes!

He answers the phone.

Kim - Yes?
Secretary - Supreme leader, Mr Trump is on the phone, he wishes to speak with you.
Kim - Transfer the call.
Donald - Kim?
Kim - Hi.
Donald - I haven't heard from you, you said you'd call.
Kim - I know… I been busy with my new 5 year plan.
Donald - How goes it?
Kim - Very well.

Donald - We need to meet. I got something for you that you'll really like.
Kim - What?
Donald - I will tell you in person. How about this weekend? I'll be in Mar-a-Lago Friday, so I could do a quick fly over and we can chat.
Kim - Okay.
Donald - Kim… would you do a big favor for me?
Kim - What?
Donald - I mean, it would really mean a lot to me.
Kim - What is it?
Donald - I'd like to meet your sister.
Kim - Really?
Donald - Yes. Both Melania and I were very impressed with the way she handled herself those 3 days she was in Seoul.
Kim - It will be my pleasure.
Donald - I'll be arriving Saturday morning. My people will be in touch with your people.
Kim - Yes.
Donald - Bye now.
Kim - Bye.

He returns to his golf game. He positions the ball carefully… measures the distance… taps the ball lightly and… in it goes!

Kim - Yes!

News item – The Washington Post reports that, according to United Nations experts, North Korea has been shipping supplies to Syria's government that could be used in the production of chemical weapons. North Korean technicians have been spotted in Syria's chemical weapons factories.

The phone rings. Kim answers.

Kim - Yes?
Secretary - Supreme leader, your Excellency, Prime Minister Putin is on the phone. He wishes to speak to you.
Kim - Transfer the call.

They speak in French.

Vladimir - Kim?
Kim - Hi.
Vladimir - Glad I could find you. You are well?
Kim (laughs) - It's funny…
Vladimir - What is?
Kim - I was just practicing my puttin' and you call.
Vladimir - What? Practicing your puttin'?
Kim - Yes, I'm getting better all the time.
Vladimir - Are you talking about golf?
Kim - Yes, what else?
Vladimir - That is not good, Kim. That is a decadent game.
Kim - No, it's not. My dad gave me once an issue of Travel and Leisure, dated 1998, and on the cover there was Fidel and Che playing golf. And they were into it.
Vladimir - Kim… I am worried about you.
Kim - Why?
Vladimir - You are letting Trump influence you.
Kim - Vladimir, we just talk, just like you and I do.
Vladimir - Do not trust that man, you will be sorry if you do. The Americans like to play games. Look what happened to poor Gaddafi in Libya. Google him, Kim, if you don't believe me, so you can see how he died. Gaddafi, the same leader who once wanted to have nuclear weapons but the Americans talked him out of it, promising that he'd be accepted in the world

community… and then they threw him to the dogs. Go ahead and google him.
Kim - I've seen it. He was killed the same year I took over… 2011. Vladimir… I'm not Gaddafi… I have a strong party behind me, something Gaddafi never built. Plus, he never got as far as I have, so do not compare me to Gaddafi.
Vladimir - Why are you meeting with him again?
Kim (surprised) - Meeting with Trump? You spying on me again?
Vladimir - Kim… I have to know. Listen… Russia gave you scientific assistance so you could build your nuclear weapons… plus we sent you oil and gas… everything… even with sanctions in place…
Kim - You did, but it's been North Korean scientists who have put things together, our own brain power that has made it happen… so don't you go now trying to steal my thunder.
Vladimir - I'm not trying to steal anything from you. All I'm trying to do is to warn you that Trump is a snake… I don't even know how he got to be president.
Kim - You don't? I thought you said your hackers had won the election for him?
Vladimir - Did I say that?
Kim - Yes, you did.
Vladimir - No, you misunderstood me, maybe a bad connection. I never said that. I had nothing to do with that. I've told Trump that. I've asked him, look into my eyes Donald, and see for yourself if you think I had anything to do with the hackers? And he did and he told me he believed me. So no, I don't deny that some Russian hackers meddled in the election, but I knew nothing about it. It was out of my control. It was reactionary Americans who elected Trump.

With his golf club still in his hand, Kim walks over to sit behind his desk.

Kim - So what is Donald going to talk to me about when he comes in to visit?
Vladimir - Calling him Donald already?
Kim - I call you by your first name. Please answer the question.
Vladimir - He's going to propose that Ivanka meet with your little sister.
Kim - Really?
Vladimir - Yep. That's the latest.
Kim - What for?
Vladimir - To advance the reunification agenda.

Kim laughs.

Vladimir - Why are you laughing?
Kim - It was me who proposed the meeting, Vladimir, and it doesn't matter what you know or don't know. Reunification will happen if I want it to happen, and you will have nothing to do with it.
Vladimir - Fool! Fool! Let the South Koreans travel freely into North Korea and they will plot to overthrow you. They will set off bombs everywhere.
Kim - Vladimir… I appreciate your concern, but I'm talking about the reunification of a nation, like the Germans did. You do not know what it is to see a nation divided. I have been ruthless, Vladimir, very ruthless, but that doesn't mean that I can't learn from my mistakes. I was very young when I came to power.
Vladimir - Fool! The only way to be sure to stay in power is to repress and repress! That's what your father did. And your grandfather, the great Kim Il-sung. Show respect for your elders, you ungrateful twit. You are there because of them. Learn from history. Repression is the only way. Stalin knew it, and Mao, and

Castro, although Castro only existed because Russia wanted a tropical island resort to go on vacation. And the people who make it through the repression, those are the truly virtuous.
Kim - Vladimir, you are talking nonsense.
Vladimir - Kim, listen to me, you idiot, Trump acts like a clown but he is a snake.
Kim - Answer me this... who would you like to see as the next American president?
Vladimir - Pence.
Kim - Really?
Vladimir - Of course. Right winger, strongly religious, perfect for us. Will keep tensions boiling and lead us back into a cold war. Both nations will have no trouble justifying a greater and greater defense budget.
Kim - But was it not your economy that couldn't keep up with America's and the Soviet Union broke up?
Vladimir - No! It was a moment of weakness. Gorbachev was duped.
Kim - Vladimir, my present political system is not sustainable. That is me being a leader, opening my eyes and seeing the truth. I owe it to my people, and even to my father and grandfather.
Vladimir - Open your borders, even a tiny bit... and you will be infiltrated by terrorists.
Kim - Are you saying that I need sanctions to survive?
Vladimir - You need sanctions to exist. Here in Russia, the sanctions have boosted my popularity, so I was able to invade and annex the Crimea. Even Gorbachev approved of it. And now I have that war going on in the Ukraine and I'm in Syria, too.
Kim - Vladimir, you have oil and gas to feed you. I don't. Sanctions are killing me. I need them lifted.
Vladimir - And what will you do about the nuclear weapons program?
Kim - I am not going to stop.

Vladimir - Good. Good. Very good. I applaud you. Are you going to export them?
Kim - I do not know.
Vladimir - Dammit, Kim, do not play games, I will not have it.
Kim - But I'm thinking of joining the community of nations…
Vladimir - What? No. It's a trap the Americans are laying out for you. Do not trust them. Are you going to export the weapons?
Kim - I do not know.
Vladimir - You'd better know or you will not survive. It's only Manchuria separating you from me, you bumpkin.
Kim - You're paranoid, Vladimir.
Vladimir - Open the borders and the power hungry Americans will organize a coup against you and have someone kill you. Like they did Gaddafi.
Kim - Vladimir… I'm not Gaddafi. What I really want is to be a statesman… not simply a dictator… Donald says I'm in transition… that I am evolving… I think I remind him of when he was young.
Vladimir - Fool! Open your eyes. Trump is poisoning your mind.
Kim - I'm thinking of being more like China. Xi is able to spy and censor his citizens and keep the economy growing.
Vladimir - The Americans will insist you give up your nuclear weapons.
Kim - I will not do that… but I know I must become more of a diplomat.
Vladimir - Why not be like us?
Kim - Your economy is not as good as the Chinese.
Vladimir - It will not last. It is a mirage. They're choking on their carbon emissions. Their air and rivers are polluted. There are going to be so many genetic mutations because of it that they will become a country of morons.
Kim - They're working on it. They're leading in solar

technology. And the Chinese military is the second largest employer in the world, behind the American military…
Vladimir (irritated) - Yes, yes, and then Walmart, and McDonald, and the National Health Service in Britain, in that order, you don't have to tell me…
Kim - You don't have to get upset that your military is not in the first five…
Vladimir - Continue, please.
Kim - … Vladimir… when the time comes… as a gesture of friendship, I will tell the world the details of when and where I will test my weapons… so they know and feel safe… and the world will be grateful… and maybe I will get invited to Berlin, to Paris, to London, to Tokyo, to Delhi, to Singapore, to Mar-a-Lago.
Vladimir - Good grief! He's got you, hasn't he?
Kim - And I will stop exporting my weapons.

Silence.

Kim - Are you there?
Vladimir - Did I hear you say… you will stop exporting your weapons?
Kim - That's right. I'm thinking about it.
Vladimir (relieved) - Well… now we're talking. That makes me feel much better. Hmm. But I'm suspicious. Those meetings with Trump are having a weird effect on you. Did he offer you a ticker tape parade in Manhattan?
Kim - Don't be ridiculous.
Vladimir - Kim, be real, don't be a sucker. The only leader likely to invite you anywhere is Maduro in Venezuela. Or Assad in Syria. Maybe Mugabe who's now in retirement will invite you for breakfast in Zimbabwe. Has Trump offered you a deal?

Kim puts the golf club on his desk, leans forward in his seat.

Kim - Vladimir… I need to ask you this… please be honest. At night… do you have ghosts come to visit you?
Vladimir - Ghosts?
Kim - Yes… ghosts of the people you've eliminated…
Vladimir - I have eliminated no one. Never poisoned anyone. Ever. There's no need for it. If there's a problem… I send some of my security people to talk to them… they have a beer together. It works all the time.
Kim - Good beer.
Vladimir - Kim… please listen… Trump is a salesman… he's selling you world participation… but no one will want you, you hear me… no one. And about your wanting to be like Xi… it's a pipe dream.
Kim - He said he would be a mentor to me…
Vladimir - Trump said that?
Kim - Yes.
Vladimir - And you believed him…? You poor thing… the blind leading the blind. Kim… listen, man… Trump can't mentor anyone… he needs a mentor.
Kim - I have to learn to trust again… baby steps.
Vladimir - I can hear Trump talking… he's got you.
Kim (irritated) - No. He does not have me. I have my nuclear weapons and I'm keeping them. It's my paranoia that has got me. Trump is right about that. It's my paranoia that has kept me isolated. That is on me. And you, Mister Vladimir, you have your own paranoia that has got you trapped - and not just you but the Russian people, too - yes, a smart and noble people like Russia, deceived and trapped by your paranoia. So I will not look to you for guidance because you do not have it in you to guide anyone.
Vladimir - Idiot! Dimwit! Imbecile! How dare you speak to me like that? After all I've done for you?

Kim - You have no belief in me... nor in your own people.

They pause for an instant.

Vladimir (calming down) - Tell you what... why don't we just take a break for now... and reset... but let me just say this... Trump... yes, the hotel owner... that snake... who fancies himself a Viking... he wants you to go to his camp... take you away from our camp... from us who have helped you stay in power... but I warn you... be careful... because you will get hurt.
And one last thing... just because your sister was all excited about being well received by South Korea, does not mean that they won't turn around and stab you in the back the moment they can. Good night.
Kim - Good night.

Kim sits back in his chair and rubs his face.

Kim - I've never spoken like that to anyone. What is happening to me? Am I thinking dangerous thoughts? Talking to the other side... just talking... has its risks. I must be careful.

3/1/18

News item - Putin announces that Russia now has nuclear armed cruise missiles. Commentators have stated that, if true, the development may alter the balance of power.
Putin stated that he had no option, given that the US had rejected existing arms control treaties and has been producing new missile defense systems.

Trump tweets - Good (Great) meeting in the Oval Office tonight with the NRA!

3/2/18

Trump tweets - Alec Baldwin, whose dying mediocre career was saved by his impersonation of me on SNL, now says playing DJT was agony for him. Alex, it was also agony for those who were forced to watch. You were terrible. Bring back Darrell Hammond, much funnier and a far greater talent!

3/3/18

Trump tweets - If the E.U. wants to increase their already massive tariffs and barriers on U.S. companies doing business there, we will simply apply a Tax on their Cars which freely pour into the U.S. They make it impossible for our cars (and more) to sell there. Big trade imbalance!

15

3/3/18

Pyongyang. North Korea.
Trump arrives for his secret meeting with Kim Jong un. Trump walks in carrying two golf clubs.

Donald - Hey, hey, how're you?
Kim - Very well. And you?
Donald - Glad to be back. Here, a present for you.

He hands Kim 2 golf clubs. Kim holds them like he has never held one before.

Donald - Oh sorry. You've never used a club?

Kim shakes his head.

Donald (showing him) - Here, this is how you hold them. Then you hit the ball so it goes in the hole.
Kim - Thank you. I download manual, read and practice.
Donald - Just so you know, this set of golf clubs has improved my game tremendously. So you're off to a great start.
Kim - Thank you, Donald.

They sit next to each other, by the coffee table.

Donald - I have some figures for you.
Kim - What?
Donald (he reads from a report) - The World Health Organization's list of countries by life expectancy. 2015 figures.

Kim - I know this. Japan number one.
Donald - They're doing something right. South Korea 11.
Kim - North Korea 109. Not good. I worry about this.
Donald - But Russia, 110. You beat them.

Kim smiles.

Donald - Congratulations. And you don't have nearly as much as they do.
Kim - How come you only 31?
Donald - We're working on it.
Kim - Cuba number 32.
Donald - That's right. We beat them.
Kim - Very narrow.
Donald - It must be the air. No industry. No pollution. Very little food, so you stay skinny.

The two men look at their paunches, then glance at each other.

Kim - You and me... too much weight.
Donald - You're right. Melania is on my case, too.
Kim - Cuba beat China, too. China number 53.
Donald - Kim... I want to help you with reunification.
Kim - You think that good for North Korea?
Donald - Good for you and the South, also. Brothers and sisters finally coming together.
Kim - But how two governments come together?
Donald - Slowly.
Kim - What system we use... democracy?
Donald - Yes.
Kim - But then people want elections.
Donald - True.
Kim (shakes his head slowly) - I not ready for that... I in

transition… transition take time… I think Chinese model better for me for now.
Donald - It's a start.

They look at each other.

Kim - You support me in transition?
Donald - Yes.

Kim smiles. Donald smiles back.

Kim - You lift sanctions?
Donald - No.
Kim - Why?
Donald - You have to earn my trust.
Kim - Baby steps?
Donald - Yes.

The two men look front as they pause.

Kim - You apply for many trademark in China.
Donald - Yes. Eventually, I'd like to see Trump hotels, golf clubs, restaurants, Trump everything, all across China. That's what I do, business. When I make money, people make money. When people make money, they are happy… and they forget. Slowly, but they forget.
Kim - What you mean?
Donald - You've had to do some things to stay in power…

Kim looks off.

Donald - You don't have to tell me. Sometimes you have been ruthless… thinking people were plotting to kill you…

Kim nods glumly.

Donald - So ghosts come around... wanting revenge.
Kim - You know about ghosts?
Donald - I do.
Kim - You eliminate some people?
Donald - Not eliminated but... disrespected, taken advantage, pushed aside, run over... groped...
Kim - Groped...?
Donald (lowering his voice) - Touched women... without consent.
Kim - Me Too movement?
Donald - Yes.
Kim - That big problem for you. I not grope.
Donald (lowering his eyes) - So I know about ghosts... and nuclear weapons can't do anything about it... they just keep coming.

Kim clasps his hands under his chin, the mood thoughtful.

Kim - How you fix problem?
Donald - Don't know yet, but I'm working on it.
Kim - What you think I do about ghosts?
Donald - Stop eliminating people. Then let people make money... and people will be happy... and they will forget.
Kim - That how Chinese model work?
Donald - I think so. A lot of people suffered in China, and some are suffering now... but there's money being made, and lots more on the way... so people learn to live with it... work around it... accept it.
Kim - One day Chinese model become democracy?
Donald - Maybe. Maybe not. It's up to the people.
Kim - No fake news.

They laugh.
Kim gets up and walks over to his desk where he turns around to face Donald.

Kim - You not plot to overthrow me?
Donald - I will not.
Kim - And when you not president?
Donald - I don't know. I can't predict. But don't worry. I'm going to get reelected and after that, Ivanka may follow me. By then, you will have made advances in your economy… got closer with the South… and become part of the world community. Your people will be happier. So why would our country want to overthrow you?
Kim - Still, I take risk.
Donald - Yes. Just like everybody else. Just like me coming over to talk to you.

Kim sits on the edge of his desk, facing Donald, looking him in the eye.

Kim - You want to speak to my sister?
Donald - Yes, very much.

Kim makes a call on his cell.

Kim - Little sister?
Little Sister (on the phone) - Yes?
Kim - You may come in.

Kim Yo Jong walks in, Donald gets up and they both shake hands.

Kim - My sister is now the new Director of the Department of

Propaganda and Agitation.

Little Sister raises her hands to her face in delighted surprise.

Donald - You've promoted her?
Kim - Yes.

Little Sister runs to embrace her brother. Then she turns to face Donald.

Donald - Congratulations. You know, as I told Melania the other day, if I had been born in your country, that's the department I would've loved to join.

And they share a laugh.

Donald (to Little Sister) - Would you like to learn how to play golf?
Little Sister - Yes.
Donald - Next time, I'll bring you a pair of clubs.
Little Sister - Thank you.
Donald - I brought your brother a pair.
Little Sister - Oh, great, he practices all the time.

Donald gives Kim a stern look, who gives a shy smile in response.

Donald (to Little Sister) - And maybe one day soon you will join me, Melania and Ivanka, at Mar-a-Lago.
Little Sister - I would like that very much.
Donald - It will be my pleasure.

16

3/4/18

The White House. Oval Office. One week later. Donald's phone rings.

Secretary - Mr President?
Donald - Yes?
Secretary - Kim Jong-un wants to speak to you.
Donald - Put him through.
Kim - Hi.
Donald - Kim, good to hear from you.
Kim - You have good trip back?
Donald - Yes. I enjoyed meeting your sister.
Kim - She enjoy meeting you.
Donald - Great.

They pause.

Donald - What's on your mind?
Kim - Donald… I appreciate the time and energy you put to meet with me secretly.
Donald - It's been a pleasure.
Kim - But I have problem.
Donald - What?
Kim - If I agree to offer… even if we announce together… it seem like your victory… you steal show.
Donald - Why do you say that?
Kim - You took first step to meet me. You look stronger than me.
Donald - Kim… you're wrong… this is a joint effort. We both

deserve credit. The fact that you built the weapons is a victory for you. So many efforts were made to have you stop and all failed. That is reality. You won but you paid a price. Your price was your isolation. Some people will see my accepting reality as a defeat for America but that is too narrow a focus. The objective now must be bringing you into the community of nations, and have you play by the rules so we don't burn up the planet.

Kim - Donald… you say you let me keep weapons but that is fact. The way you say it… that you are 'letting me' keep weapons, make you look like you stronger than Kim.

Donald - We can change the language… maybe say, 'the USA recognizes North Korea is now a nuclear power', how about that?

Kim - Better. Now, if you lift some sanctions…

Donald - No.

They're quiet for a moment.

Kim - Donald, I cannot look weaker than you.

Donald - You're not looking weaker than me.

Kim - Donald, secret meeting is good because I get to know you… but I think it is best to have big meeting… tell the world in advance… then everybody talk about meeting… and your people and my people meet and talk for 2-3 days… and we will be in newspapers all over the world… and then you and me come to final meeting…

Donald - Big show. Political theater.

Kim - And then you make big offer… you recognize me as nuclear power… in big meeting… not in secret. And I will announce that I let world know when I test missile… and I make commitment to not export nuclear weapon.

Donald - I see… but Kim… I will not lift the sanctions until I trust you.

They pause.

Donald - Kim… we have been so close to making a deal… what's happened?
Kim - I afraid…
Donald - Afraid of what…?
Kim - World community not accept me…
Donald - It's going to take a while… but I will be your mentor… I will introduce you…
Kim - You want me to trust you?
Donald - Yes.
Kim - I take risk.
Donald - We both do.

They're quiet again.

Kim - You agree to have big meeting… say to world I am nuclear power?
Donald - Okay.
Kim - Then I agree to live with sanction. Until you trust me. And I say to world, 'I have to prove that North Korea is responsible…that we don't make threats to bomb another country… that we don't export weapon… that we learn not to live in fear'.
Donald - Well said. Deal.
Kim - And nobody know about secret meeting?
Donald - Deal.
Kim - Except Putin.

They laugh.

Donald - He knows everything.
Kim - Thank you, Donald.

Donald - You're most welcome.

3/6/18

Kim Jong-un meets in Pyongyang with South Korean delegates. Kim said that he was open to talking to Washington about ending his nuclear weapons program, would suspend their development while talks took place and would accept the US -South Korean military exercises. A meeting with President Moon Jae-in was set for April.

3/6/18

Trump tweets – The new Fake News narrative is that there is CHAOS in the White House. Wrong! People will always come and go, and I want strong dialogue before making a final decision. I still have some people that I want to change (always seeking perfection). There is no Chaos, only great Energy!

3/8/18

South Korean envoys met with President Trump at the White House, to report on their conversation with Kim Jong-un. The envoys stated that the North Korean leader was committed to denuclearization and that he was eager to meet with Trump. Mr Trump accepted. A tentative date was set for May.
The talks would be a meeting, not a negotiation
President Trump added that no sanctions will be lifted until an agreement is reached.

17

3/9/18

Washington DC. The White House. The Oval office. / Moscow. The Kremlin.
Donald is seated at his desk.
He tweets - Look forward to being in Pennsylvania tomorrow in support of Rick Saccone. Big crowd expected in Moon Township. Vote Rick and see you there!

His cell phone rings.

Secretary - Mr President?
Donald - Yes?
Secretary - Vladimir Putin would like to speak to you?
Donald - Sure. Put him through.
Vladimir - Donald…
Donald - Vladimir…
Vladimir - Well, well… old Kim finally got you to the negotiating table, didn't he?
Donald - He did.
Vladimir - You were doing quite well, there, for a while, in your secret talks, and then he switched up on you.

Pause.

Donald - Not so secret, were they?
Vladimir - Ah, forgive me, Donald…. but it's hard for an old KGB hand to give up his tricks.
Of course, you're free to spy on me as you wish. If you have the

technology.

Donald - We have it. We know more than you imagine, to be used when necessary.

Vladimir - Don't worry, I will not reveal what you had been trying to do. In fact, I thank you for making an effort to persuade Kim.

Donald - You think I did?

Vladimir - Maybe. He just needs to have his moment in the limelight, but you hold the pieces. In the end, he'll have to back off.

Donald - It's not over yet…

Vladimir - We can live with him having the weapons.

Donald - Of course. By the way, thank you for putting pressure on him.

Vladimir - What pressure?

Donald - To not export the nuclear weapons.

Vladimir - How did you…?

Donald - Like I said, we have our ways.

Vladimir - I'm surprised.

Vladimir - And the military exercises with South Korea?

Donald - We'll resume them shortly… and keep doing them till the end of time.

Donald gets up from behind his desk and goes to sit by the fireplace.

Donald - We're still not clear as to the exact position of all his missiles… are you?

Vladimir - We're not.

Donald - Between your capabilities and ours, we should be able to do it… what do you think?

Vladimir - Team work?

Donald - Indeed.

Vladimir - Are you asking?
Donald - Yes.
Vladimir - Well… considering that you have made an effort to reach him… I don't see why we can't work together.
Donald - That way we keep Kim honest. And the world community will be grateful.
Vladimir - It will be nice to be acknowledged instead of being seen as a monster.
Donald - I know the feeling. We'll have to keep it secret, though.
Vladimir - Of course. I meant, by the history books.
Donald - Yes. What did you think of Mueller's indictments?
Vladimir - Like I've told you, I've had nothing to do with it. I try to monitor as much as I can but it's not possible to identify every hacker.
Donald - They took advantage of our polarized politics.
Vladimir - Like you Americans say, it was easy pickings.

Donald picks up a secret briefing from the coffee table and thumbs through it.

Vladimir - I've never told you this, but when I first saw you in action – during the campaign - I didn't think you had a chance. But when the networks televising the debates kept putting you in the center of the podium… and your adversaries were not refuting you strongly, I thought, the man has a chance.
Donald - The ratings would go up with each debate. Reflecting back on it, I find it interesting that my experience in a TV show – The Apprentice – was critical to my becoming president.
Vladimir - A sign of the times. A 'made for TV' president.

Donald laughs.

Donald - Vladimir, had Hillary won, would you have been able to get along?

Vladimir - We would have. She would have ranted and raved for a while… but then she would've settled down and talked. What other choice is there?

Donald - True.

Vladimir - You can't go on moralizing ad infinitum. The world is what it is.

Donald - Which reminds me of Syria. We dropped the ball there. You know, if I had been president, instead of Obama, I would've bombed the hell out of Assad after his first chemical weapons assault.

Vladimir - I'm sure you would have… and who knows what Syria would look like now because I would not have backed down.

Donald - I think we would have seized the advantage and you would've had trouble selling a greater war commitment to your people.

Vladimir - You don't think you would've had resistance at home? You're spread thin as it is – with all those troops in Afghanistan and Iraq. It gets expensive.

Donald - Draining blood and treasure. I can't believe Bush got us into Iraq.

Vladimir - I don't think you're ever getting out. Of course, I could make things easier for you in Syria, but then I would lose standing in the area, and appearances matter.

Donald - Having Iran's approval is important?

Vladimir - Being a player is important. Speaking of which, Netanyahu came over the other day.

Donald - He's done it often.

Vladimir - Sadly, his days are counted. I think the bribery charges will bring him down.

Donald - There may be a way around it. You don't have that problem, do you?

Vladimir - I'm careful… but it helps to have influence over the judiciary and the press.
Donald - Nice.
Vladimir - I'll be sorry to see Bibi leave.
Donald - So will I. How did you like my decision to make Jerusalem the capital?
Vladimir - Surprised me.
Donald - Escaped your spies, didn't we?
Vladimir - Yes.
Donald - I had promised my Jewish backers.
Vladimir - Of course. Are you going to keep sending weapons to Ukraine?
Donald - I have to. As you say, being a player is important.
Vladimir - At your risk. Draining blood and treasure.
Donald - It won't last forever. As tensions escalate, and you and I make a greater weapons commitment, I don't think your economy will be able to sustain it, not with the sanctions in place.
Vladimir - We're in a different place than in Reagan's day. The price of commodities is up, and we have plenty of oil and gas to sell.
Donald - Until renewables come around… but that'll be awhile.
Vladimir - My ratings are at an all time high. Russians don't mind a bit of suffering.
Donald - How long do you want to stay in power?
Vladimir - As long as I'm able. I like it up here.
Donald - I wish I could say the same.
Vladimir - Are you running again?
Donald - Yes. I like it up here, too. Speaking of which, don't you love what Xi pulled off?
Vladimir - The man has got the touch.
Donald - He'll die in office. I'm envious.

They laugh.

Vladimir - You think you'll win the next time around?
Donald - The Left is doing the work for me. They're so strident in their opposition that when you read the news, it's like I can't do anything right. Not that I haven't made my mistakes, but people will tire of the constant badgering and they'll become sympathetic. You think I'll win?
Vladimir - You have a chance.
Donald - Do me a favor and make sure there's no Russians involved in the election.
Vladimir - Donald, I have no control over all Russians, though most people think I do, but I give you my promise that I will do my very best.
Donald - Thank you.

Putin gets up and paces around in his office.

Vladimir - After your second term, you will be done?
Donald - Yes.
Vladimir - What will you do afterwards?
Donald - Go back to New York. Back to my hotels. Travel the world with a secret service detail. Give speeches. The Trump Show. Maybe go back to TV. Can't beat that, can you?
Vladimir - Ah, yes. You have that.
Donald - They love me in India. In China, too. You envious?
Vladimir - A little. It's unlikely I'll ever be part of the lecture circuit, getting a quarter million dollars for a speech. There will be hysterical protesters outside, holding placards saying 'Go Home Putin!' Or some other obnoxious thing.
Donald - I'm sure you're set.
Vladimir - I'll do fine. Mother Russia will see to it. All those years of service.
Donald - Look, it's not too late to be thinking of a chain of hotels…

Vladimir (laughs) - Never had any interest.
Donald - C'mon, be honest….
Vladimir - Never have. Truly.
Donald - How about a round of golf?
Vladimir - Now that, I've been thinking about lately. I love swimming and horseback riding but learning to golf might be interesting.
Donald - You can swim and golf at Mar-a-Lago. Would you like to come?
Vladimir - Sure.
Donald - Once the Mueller investigation is done, I'll have you over for a weekend. You'll love it. Once you see it, you'll want to have one of your own. Think of it as a retirement thing.
Vladimir - I'm fine, really, Mother Russia will be there for me, but that's thoughtful of you.
Donald - You're welcome.
Vladimir - Well, I won't keep you longer.
Donald - Vladimir… if evidence is found that you knew about the hacking of the election… I will have to come down hard on you.
Vladimir - I understand… but like I've said before, nothing will be found.
Donald - I hope so.

They pause for a moment.

Vladimir - Donald… about the Mueller investigation…
Donald - Yes…
Vladimir - Just a view from afar… I'm sure you're not guilty of collusion… but the way you react to what Mueller is doing or not doing… it sure looks like you're hiding something.
Donald - I'm really upset about all the money being wasted… that's all.

Vladimir - Of course.
Donald - I'm curious. What're people saying over there?
Vladimir - Well… you haven't shown your taxes… and then the way you react… so some people are saying that Mueller will find that you're not as rich as you say you are.
Donald - Hogwash. Believe me… I'm very rich. Very.
Vladimir - You should relax a little about that… so what if you're not? You're in power, Donald… and you have shown that you can make it count.
Donald - Thank you, Vladimir.
Vladimir - You're welcome.

18

The White House.
Same day. Evening. Presidential suite.
Donald and Melania are seated at the table, a bottle of fine cider and two half filled glasses next to them.

Melania - It's too bad. You and Kim were getting so close…
Donald - So it appeared…
Melania - But it's not over…
Donald - … till it's over.

They smile at each other.
Melania picks up her glass and raises it for a toast.

Donald - What are we celebrating?
Melania - Here's to your trying as you did.
Donald - I'll drink to that.

They clink and sip.

Melania - Have you thought of making a public announcement about the way you mistreated women?
Donald - I have. It's been on my mind.
Melania - What would you say?
Donald - You ready?
Melania - Yes.
Donald - I've actually worked on this.
Melania - Let's hear it.
Donald - To all of the women whom I have mistreated… I beg your forgiveness. In my fits of narcissism… I have violated your

boundaries... treated you like chattel... thought myself entitled to your bodies to suit my carnal desires. Owning up to my transgressions... is an acknowledgement of the predator impulse in me... a first step to understanding it... and to control it... for I have caused emotional injuries that have left you with scars. I have no doubt that... with the assistance of my wife Melania... and maybe a psychiatrist... I will, in time, conquer that disgraceful flaw in my character... and help me move toward becoming a better human being... and a better man.

Melania raises her glass again.

Melania - And a better president.

They clink and sip.

Melania - You really want me to help you?
Donald - I do.
Melania - Then I will.
Donald - Thank you, dear.

He rises and extends his hand to her.

Donald - Would you like to dance?
Melania - Yes.

She rises and they embrace.

Donald (singing softly as he leads her in dance) - Love... is a many splendored thing...

And they glide toward the window and the moonlight shining through.

The End

Thanks to Ann Altmark for reading the manuscript.

www.ingramcontent.com/pod-product-compliance
Lightning Source LLC
Chambersburg PA
CBHW020653300426
44112CB00007B/368